THE BATTLE-TESTED GUIDE
TO GOAL ACHIEVEMENT

OBJECTIVE SECURE

NICK LAVERY

Objective Secure: The Battle-Tested Guide to Goal Achievement
Published by Precision Components LLC.
Brooklyn, New York

Copyright ©2022 by Nick Lavery. All rights reserved.

No part of this book may be reproduced in any form or by any
mechanical means, including information storage and retrieval
systems without permission in writing from the publisher/author,
except by a reviewer who may quote passages in a review.

All images, logos, quotes, and trademarks included in this book are
subject to use according to trademark and copyright laws of the
United States of America.

ISBN: 978-0-578-35201-5
BIOGRAPHY & AUTOBIOGRAPHY / Military
SELF-HELP / Motivational & Inspirational

Interior design by Victoria Wolf, wolfdesignandmarketing.com.
Cover design by Ray Vermiglio. Copyright owned by Nick Lavery.

All rights reserved by Nick Lavery and Precision Components LLC.
Printed in the United States of America.

CONTENTS

AUTHOR'S INTENT

MISSION: Reader will absorb the principles and vignettes of *Objective Secure* at times and locations suitable for maximum focus in order to enhance perspective and facilitate achievement.

EXPANDED PURPOSE: *Objective Secure* was developed to enable those striving toward a goal, those who perceive a goal unobtainable, and those struggling to determine a goal.

KEY TASKS:[1]
+ Read
+ Ruminate
+ Implement

END STATE: Reader has unlocked pre-existing potential. Reader is equipped with a newly acquired series of tools and methodology. Reader recognizes anything is possible with an effective mindset and strategy. Reader employs the *Objective Secure* system and philosophy, resulting in sustained determination, progress, and inspiration to others.

---

1   Activities necessary to achieve the desired end state.

SPY PROM

AUGUST, 2019. Upon notification that I was being nominated for the Office of Strategic Services (OSS) Society's Peter Ortiz Award, I didn't give it much thought. My team and I were in the middle of a robust training cycle in preparation for deployment, and my focus was on the mission. A few weeks later, upon notification I would be receiving the award, I finally did some research. I learned that Colonel Peter Ortiz was the most decorated member of the OSS. Not only that, he was a total badass. To be presented an award in his name was an absolute honor. I struggled to craft an acceptance speech. I felt my name belonged nowhere near that of Peter Ortiz. Once it set in that I wouldn't be up on that stage alone, that I was merely a representation of something much bigger and more significant, receipt of this honor became much easier to accept. With my father and wife by my side, we arrived at our nation's capital.

On October 12, 2019, in the Washington, DC, Ritz-Carlton's grand ballroom, the OSS Society hosted its annual gala officially known as the William J. Donovan Award Dinner. "The hottest party you've never heard of" remains absent from the standard list of must-attend Washington social events where members of the intelligence and special operations communities come together to recognize those who have exemplified the distinguishing features of the honor's namesake, the World War II general known as "Wild Bill" Donovan. With a live orchestra softly playing the works of Frank Sinatra and Dean Martin, more than eight hundred attendees in tuxedos, gowns, and full-dress military uniforms sip martinis, converse, and sway on the dance floor. The only thing missing from what is unofficially dubbed "Spy Prom" is 007 raking in chips at the baccarat table.

The awards presented during this esteemed event include the William J. Donovan Award, the Hugh Montgomery Award, the Virginia Hall Award, and, finally, the Peter Ortiz Award, which on this night was presented by the commander of the United States Army Special Operations Command (USASOC), Lieutenant General Francis M. Beaudette:

"Ladies and gentlemen, it is my absolute honor to be here tonight to introduce one of our very best, Warrant Officer Nick Lavery. He is a special operator in whom Wild Bill Donovan would immediately recognize the calculated recklessness and disciplined daring he saw in his generation of warriors. On behalf of our four thousand Army Special Operations warriors deployed today, thank you all for your stalwart support of our men and women, and especially of our cherished Gold Star families. You truly make a difference to all of them. Thank you. [applause]

"Simply put, Warrant Officer Nick Lavery is a warrior's warrior. Nick selflessly and repeatedly risked his life for his nation, his comrades in arms, and, most importantly, he accomplished what our nation needed him to do every time he left our shores. Nick is a hero in the truest sense, and I am incredibly humbled and proud that you are honoring him here tonight.

Thank you to the OSS Society for bestowing this recognition to Nick, and having Nick's family here tonight is truly special. Thank you to Mike and Toni for celebrating this with us. It is great to spend time with you. [applause]

"Nick's chosen profession requires an emersion into some of the nation's most difficult challenges, often in demanding, complex, and especially uncertain environments. To answer the nation's call, we seek men and women who have the tenacity to achieve the impossible and the resiliency to do it again and again. Nick Lavery's story is truly an exemplar of that.

"Two thousand and twelve was just another year of dangerous living for Nick. In September, he took shrapnel to his back during a village clearing operation in Afghanistan. In November, he was shot in the face while rescuing his detachment commander from a burning vehicle in a complex ambush. But each time he refused to be evacuated out of country for his wounds, insisting that he return to his detachment, which he did. This is typical Nick.

"In 2013, things got tougher. On March 11, he found himself under withering machine-gun fire during an insider attack. Nick, being the incredible, selfless, and especially brave Green Beret that he is, rushed out to save an American infantryman caught in the open during the ambush. In doing so, Nick was shot five times. His significant wounds ultimately resulted in the amputation of his right leg above the knee. As you could imagine, Nick was in a tough spot and had a long and demanding recovery in front of him. But his grit and raw determination kept him going, and again he insisted on returning to his detachment despite being told he'd have a tough time walking down a grocery store aisle.

"Over time, he regained his superhuman strength—and with this I am really not kidding. He is, in fact, that strong for an average-sized human being. [laughter] He requested a team assignment; leading from the front as usual, Nick demanded that he earn his spot. He prepared for the operational readiness test, an incredibly rigorous series of aerobic and anaerobic physical requirements that replicate the challenges of combat. Nick passed, and was the first above-the-knee amputee to do so.

"Upon return to the 3rd Special Forces Group, [Nick served] first as a lead instructor for the Special Operations Combatives Program, where, legend has it, he greatly increased the lethality of Green Berets while frankly terrifying anybody who had to fight him. [laughter]

"Nick, once fully healed, quickly got back to his team, and that same incredible determination led him back to Afghanistan, becoming again the first Special Forces operator to return to combat as an above-the-knee amputee. After two additional combat deployments on a team, Nick's warrior mindset and desire for continued selfless service led him to commission as a Special Forces Warrant Officer, where he remains on the line to this day, making a difference.

"The key to the success of the OSS was the great talent within the people who served. Since then, nothing has changed. Our people make us the force that we are, generating options for the nation regardless of the hard problem. Nick is indeed very special, and he remains one of our most inspiring examples. His refusal to quit in the face of adversity, his gallantry, his outstanding leadership, his professionalism, and his personal courage are the standards our warriors strive to attain.

"Nick would make General Donovan as proud as we are of him. The men and women of special operations like Nick Lavery are in demanding places serving on the forward edge of freedom.

Whether in Afghanistan, Syria, or abroad addressing other threats to our national security, our soldiers are present, they are capable, and they are representing American values around the world each and every day. I assure you, men and women like Nick are in places all over where we need them to be. They will continue to contribute to our nation's credible deterrence, and when called upon, they are going to fight and win as part of the joint force alongside our allies and partners. When the time comes, our men and women will prevail in competition or in war, through daring determination, precise lethality, and agile creativity, just like Nick.

"These are the hallmarks of service in special operations exemplified tonight by the actions and integrity of Nick Lavery. Now, we don't have a cool guy drink,[2] but we have warriors like Nick Lavery. Go, Army! [laughter and cheers]

"Please help me welcome to the podium Green Beret Warrant Officer Nick Lavery." [standing ovation]

2   If you weren't at the event, you wouldn't get the joke.

*LTG Beaudette presenting the Peter Ortiz Award
to Nick, Washington, DC, October 12, 2019*[3]

FOREWORD

THE GREATEST HONOR OF MY LIFE has been serving alongside the freedom-loving Americans of Army special operations—men and women like Nick Lavery—who willingly accept the most dangerous missions on behalf of the nation with daring determination. The storied legacy of the Green Berets was forged in battle by the deeds of these courageous warriors, and I will forever be grateful for their service.

I've seen firsthand that freedom isn't free; it is paid for by the sacrifices of our country's finest sons and daughters. Every day our cherished Gold Star families, whose loved ones gave their lives for the nation, inspire us with their grace and strength. We, too, owe much to our combat veterans who selflessly and repeatedly risk their lives for the mission and for their comrades in arms. Many return from war with visible or invisible injuries, and the road to recovery can be daunting.

But what our Soldiers can do in the face of adversity is simply remarkable. When Nick lost his leg, he attacked rehabilitation as he would any mission, with humility, hard work, and tenacity. What's unique about special operations forces is our ability to seize opportunity, even when it seems impossible to everyone else. Nick's approach was no exception. He never retreated. He just attacked in another direction.

The key to America's success is the great talent of Americans who choose to serve. Nick is very special and he remains one of Army special operations' most inspiring examples. The power of Nick's story is not found solely in his monumental achievements—which are extraordinary—it's in the simplicity of his process and his genuine desire to help his teammates. Through his experiences (and an Army special operations trade secret or two), he shows you in *Objective Secure* how to conquer your impossible.

Nick's book is a tribute to all of our warriors whose grit, resilience, and indomitable spirit keep them going regardless of the challenges they face. May we model their bravery under hardship and have their courage in crisis.

Lieutenant General Fran Beaudette[4]
February 22, 2021

---

4   The views presented in this foreword are my own and do not necessarily represent the views of the Department of Defense or its components.

INTRODUCTION

Objective:

1. the clearly defined, decisive, and attainable goal toward which every operation is directed

2. the specific target of the action taken (for example, a definite terrain feature, the seizure or holding of which is essential to the commander's plan, or an enemy force or capability without regard to terrain features). See also *target* (JP 3-0) (US DOD)

Objective Secure: a military brevity term used during the execution of combat operations meaning the location or target has been isolated and contained, the assault force has eliminated all known threats, and the element is prepared to move to the next objective or phase of the operation.

When you dream, what do you see? What do you want most? Who do you want to become? For some, this is a possession: the perfect

1

family home, perhaps a boat. For others, this is professional: a new position at work, maybe a promotion, or perhaps a new career altogether. Some seek a transformation within themselves: a decrease in body fat, more muscle mass. Maybe it's living without pain or gaining increased intelligence, understanding, or self-actualization. Perhaps it is something social: a better relationship with a spouse or parent or child. Whatever it is, allow yourself to focus on it.

I, of course, don't know what your dream is. I have no idea how insurmountable it may seem. But what I do know is this: Chances are it's going to be difficult; obstacles and adversity are almost certain. But whatever it is, it is possible.

Everybody wants to be great at something. Great at a job. Great at a skill. Great as a parent, spouse, coach, or friend. The unfortunate reality, however, is that, for most, this greatness will remain nothing more than a dream because desire alone produces nothing.

Fear not. Average gradually becomes easier to accept. The rationalizations, the justifications, the lies we tell ourselves, the excuses, our lifestyle, our "needs," our parents, our children—these become options (among others) to enable our acceptance of average, our "reasons" we "can't" do more, be more. Over time, we condition ourselves to the point where mediocre becomes our ceiling.

Have you ever just stopped and asked yourself, "At what point did I place these limitations on myself? When did I determine I couldn't do something?" The classic story of the elephant and the rope addresses this superbly. The short version is a man was walking past a group of circus elephants. Each was being held by a single rope tied from its leg to a stake in the ground. The man asked the trainer why these enormous animals didn't simply break away. Obviously they had the strength to do so. The trainer responded by saying that when the elephants are very young and much weaker, their trainers use the same rope and stake to hold them. At first they struggle and fight to break free, but the rope and stake are strong enough to hold them. Eventually the elephants stop trying to break free.

Sound familiar? Something you can relate to? It certainly is for me. No problem. We simply must recognize it. And now that we have addressed the elephant in the room (insert laughing face emoji), hear this: every single moment is an opportunity to pivot, to break free, or, better yet, to break through.

The specific reasons for picking up this book will vary between individuals, but I believe that for all, it comes from a feeling within—a feeling that there is more to achieve, that average sucks, that anything is possible. A feeling that tells us that going through life unhappy, without passion, and enduring daily dissatisfaction is not living at all. Congratulations! This feeling is the beginning of something called growth. You have just taken the first step.

Welcome to *Objective Secure*.

THE SPECIAL FORCES OPERATIONAL DETACHMENT-ALPHA (a.k.a. SFOD-A, or simply ODA) is the nomenclature for a Special Forces (SF) team. The leadership structure on the team is a tripod consisting of the detachment commander, the operations sergeant, and the warrant officer.

The detachment commander—a.k.a. team leader (TL) or Alpha (the Military Occupational Specialty or MOS[5] for an SF officer—is 18A). This individual holds the rank of captain and is ultimately in charge. Everybody on the team answers to the team leader. He is

---

5   A soldier's MOS is essentially his or her job in the Army.

responsible for (among other things) determining *what* the team is going to do. He is the face of the team—the leader.

The operations sergeant, a.k.a. team sergeant or Zulu (MOS 18Z), runs the team. Aside from the leadership, ODAs are composed entirely of noncommissioned officers (NCOs). Every NCO on the team works for the team sergeant. He is the most senior enlisted member on the team, typically a master sergeant, and is hands down the most influential individual on the team. He is responsible for (among other things) determining *how* the team is going to accomplish the team leader's desired end state—the boss.

The warrant officer, a.k.a. assistant detachment commander (ADC) or chief (MOS 180A), holds the rank of warrant officer one through chief warrant officer two.[6] The warrant is responsible for (among other things) long-range training management, risk management, and mission planning. The warrant typically has the most time spent on an ODA. His experience enables his real functions: advisor and confidant. He is the "consigliere" (e.g., Tom Hagen in *The Godfather*).

Special Forces warrants learn and employ a variety of systems, tools, and methodologies to assist their function: systems that help organize thought, tools that help define a situation, and methodology that helps synchronize multiple efforts in the pursuit of a single outcome. The Special Forces warrant uses these methods to paint a clear picture and advise the commander accordingly.

This is *Objective Secure*.

Reaching Objective Secure during a combat operation is a good feeling. It means we have a foothold—a location to reconsolidate, establish communications, prepare, stage, and, if necessary, fall back to. But this does not mean the mission is complete.

6   On extremely rare occasions, Chief Warrant Officer Three.

Objective Secure in our context here is twofold. First, it is a victory, a milestone. It marks the success of achieving a necessary goal along the route to mission accomplishment. Second, it is a tool, a system, a methodology—a process designed to manifest our reality. Objective Secure is a philosophy and a blueprint that was created in real time, refined, then retrospectively analyzed following years of trial and error, years of failure, years of obstacles, and years of adversity. It was forged by fire and is battle-tested—literally.

MY NAME IS NICK LAVERY. Born and raised in Massachusetts, I am an active-duty member of the United States Army Special Forces, more commonly referred to as the Green Berets. After graduating from college with a bachelor's degree in criminal justice, I enlisted in the Army in 2007 as a Special Forces recruit (MOS 18x), a contract option that gives recruits the opportunity to enter directly into the SF pipeline. Upon completion of a long list of training to include One Station Unit Training,[7] Airborne School, Special Forces Assessment and Selection (SFAS), and the Special Forces Qualification Course (SFQC), which all in all took over two years, I became a Green Beret.

On my second combat deployment to Afghanistan in 2012, I was wounded in action on three separate occasions. The first was just a few weeks after getting into country, when I was hit with some shrapnel in the back of my shoulder during a village clearance operation. It was suggested I be medically evacuated (MedEvac) out of country

---

7   One Station Unit Training (OSUT) refers to a training program in which recruits remain with the same unit for both Basic Combat Training and Advanced Individual Training (AIT). AIT is where new Soldiers receive specific training for the chosen MOS.

for medical treatment. I refused. The second was a couple of months later, when I was shot in the face while extracting our detachment commander from a burning truck following an improvised explosive device (IED)-initiated ambush. Once again, medical evacuation from country was suggested, and once again, I refused.

With approximately three weeks left in our deployment, I was shot five times during an insider attack—four times in my right leg and once in my lower left. The MedEvac bird (helicopter) couldn't land during the ongoing ambush, so I was forced to wait over an hour to be airlifted out. With my femur shattered and my femoral artery severed, I should have died that day. Instead, my injuries ultimately resulted in the amputation of my right leg above the knee.

I spent a year at Walter Reed Medical Center undergoing more than thirty surgeries and learning how to live with a prosthetic before returning to my unit, where I was offered a full medical military retirement. I refused. I was then assigned to our Advanced Skills Company (ASC), where I worked as an instructor teaching close-quarters battle (CQB) and hand-to-hand combat on the Special Operations Combatives Program (SOCP) committee while continuing my rehabilitation. After approximately eight months, I decided I was ready to pursue returning to operational status—something that, although supported by my chain of command, family, and friends, few felt was actually possible. This was certainly understandable given the severity of my injuries and the physical rigors of the job.

Over a three-month period, I went through a tough series of physical, psychological, cognitive, and proficiency evaluations and assessments orchestrated to determine my capability. Our chain of command would be assuming an enormous, unprecedented risk by putting me back onto an ODA. This decision would be scrutinized by senior leadership, and they needed to be confident I could perform as required. At the conclusion, I was given the green light[8] to return to my team. Two months later, I was back in Afghanistan with my detachment conducting combat operations.

From point of injury to returning to combat was right around two years in total, and I am considered the first Special Forces operator to return to combat as an above-the-knee amputee. I have since deployed to combat multiple times to other areas in the Middle East and Africa, and back in May 2019 I transitioned to become an SF warrant officer, the first amputee to do so in military history.

I remain on an ODA to this day, where I serve as the assistant detachment commander (ADC). I am blessed to belong to a profession I love, and I will remain doing what we do for as long as I am able, or, more accurately, for as long as I am an asset.

I REALIZE THAT WAS BRIEF AND SUPERFICIAL. I am certain you have questions, many of which will be addressed in the pages to come. However, let's quickly examine the two I am asked most frequently, and ones you may be asking yourself: the why and the how.

WHY?

"Why do you continue doing this given what you have endured? Haven't you sacrificed enough?"

The why is easy to answer.

For one, I am extremely competitive. And while I love to win, I really hate to lose, and there's a difference. I grew up playing sports. I played football in college, so from a young age I developed

---

8 Approval.

a competitive spirit that remains to this day. Nobody was going to determine my fate other than me. Nobody.

I attribute my stubbornness and competitiveness as key traits that kept me alive. The same reasons why I refused to be medically evacuated from Afghanistan after my first two injuries, the same reason why I refused to die after the third, and the same reason why I refused medical retirement is part of the same reason why I still do this today. I hate to lose.

In addition to that, I love what I do. An expression I am sure everybody is familiar with says that if you love what you do you will never work a day in your life. Well, in this context, I rarely work. Yes, there are days when I feel like I am working. But, on most days, I feel privileged. Because that's what it is. It is a privilege to work alongside such unbelievable individuals and serve on behalf of the American people. At the end of the day, we work for the citizens of the United States, and that is something I take extremely seriously.

I swore an oath to defend the United States. That is a contract I must live up to. And as long as I am able to perform at the highest level, as long as I am considered an asset and provide value, I have a responsibility to live up to my end of the bargain. I can, so I must—period.

HOW?

"How do you function on a team as a Green Beret with only one leg? How did the Army allow that? How do you do it?"

The how is a bit more complex. This is something that initially was fluid in nature. I essentially made it up as I went along. Although I had many people in my corner—family, friends, colleagues, coaches, mentors—ultimately, I had to figure it out on my own. That is the price for doing something that has never been done before.

I simply made a decision. It was scary and painful, and I could not see the light at the end of the tunnel, because I wasn't in a tunnel at all. It wasn't some straight path. In fact, I wasn't on any sort of previously established route at all. I was moving uphill along a jagged, windy mountainside in the darkness surrounded by obstacles, and although I couldn't see the light at the end, I knew it was there. We know this as faith.

Faith:
1. allegiance to duty or a person
2. firm belief in something for which there is no proof
3. something that is believed especially with strong conviction (*Merriam-Webster*)

Anybody or anything that stood in my way was removed from the equation, and I attacked my initial rehabilitation, the training that followed, and the redefining of myself like an absolute lunatic. I was relentless. I was unreasonable. Because I felt that's what it took. That *is* what it takes.

Objective Secure is ultimately the answer to this question.

Objective Secure is a hybrid—the combination of art and science, the mind and the body, the yin and the yang, the theoretical and the tangible. It is a guide that enables our pursuit for excellence, for greatness, for success, no matter what stands in our way.

So strap in, keep all hands and feet inside the vehicle and remain seated at all times. Let's go.

MINDSET

Mindset:

1. a mental attitude or inclination
2. a fixed state of mind (*Merriam-Webster*)

First let's discuss the conceptual side, the abstract. Here we will focus on the mindset necessary to reach mission success—a warrior mindset.

AUGUST 13, 2007, was my first day in the United States Army. It began at the 30th Adjutant General (Reception) Battalion (a.k.a. 30th AG), located on Ft. Benning, Georgia. This is the first location US Army basic training recruits arrive at prior to the actual start of basic training. Its purpose is to receive, prepare, and train personnel for what lies ahead. While I am sure we were given some classes, the only things I recall during my time at 30th AG were doing paperwork, eating our three meals a day, and waiting—a lot of waiting, most of which was spent standing in formation.

We stood in formation for hours each day. While in formation, waiting, for what seemed like an eternity, we would "sound off" (say loudly) with several mantras. The Soldier's Creed, the Army Song, and the Warrior Ethos are a few that come to mind. At any point, a drill sergeant, a member of the command, or any Soldier in the formation would simply yell "The Warrior Ethos" (for example). Then the entire formation of Soldiers would sound off with that mantra. This served two purposes. One, it killed time, even if it was only thirty seconds of time. It gave us something to do. Two, it ingrained these mantras into our heads. Basic training is the Army's method to break down an individual into human clay in order to then be remolded into a Soldier. The same goes for the other branches of the military. The verbalization of mantras is part of that process. The Warrior Ethos was one of them.

The term *warrior* is pretty self-explanatory. A warrior is a soldier or fighter, someone familiar with warfare.

Warrior:

1. a person engaged or experienced in warfare
2. a person engaged in some struggle or conflict
(*Merriam-Webster*)

The term *ethos* is derived from the same Greek root as *ethics*, meaning principles of conduct governing an individual or group.

Ethos:

1. the distinguishing character, sentiment, moral nature, or guiding beliefs of a person, group, or institution (*Merriam-Webster*)

The Army's Warrior Ethos is a code of conduct—ideals by which every soldier lives. In a broader sense, the Warrior Ethos is a way of life. It defines who we are and who we aspire to become, but it is most certainly not exclusive to those of us who are warriors by profession. This way of life—the warrior mindset—is an option for literally everybody.

The Warrior Ethos has four tenets:

1. I will always place the mission first.
2. I will never accept defeat.
3. I will never quit.
4. I will never leave a fallen comrade.

We are going to use these tenets to provide structure. Here we go...

I WILL ALWAYS PLACE
THE MISSION FIRST.

NOW I REALIZE the term *mission* has a strong military undertone, but this absolutely applies to everybody, because everybody has dreams. That's what the mission is. It's the dream. The long-term goal. The mission is what is waiting at the end of the road. Missions are impactful—often life-changing—but for many, the mission will remain just that, a dream. Many do not reach mission success. Many do not turn the dream into a reality. Those who do are able to recognize the need for something—*sacrifice*—a subset of discipline (something we will get into later), the act of forgoing what we want for what we need.

Sacrifice:
1. something given up or lost (*Merriam-Webster*)

———————

AS A CHILD AND A TEEN, I moved around a lot. In fact, it wasn't until I entered college that I lived in the same place for longer than eighteen months. This was tough. I was constantly the new kid. I struggled to make friends. And to make matters more difficult, I was tiny. What would today be classified as bullying was just kids being kids back then. Athletics provided me an outlet. It was something I excelled at; therefore, I used sports as my anchor. With that grew a passion for physical training, and my desire to become big and strong was twofold. It would help me in sports and it would also minimize me being picked on. The Incredible Hulk was never picked on. Mike Singletary wasn't scared to ride the bus. Hulk Hogan had more friends than he knew what to do with.

When I was around nine years old, my parents bought me a dumbbell set. It had pairs of three-, five-, and eight-pounders. I began constantly working out in my bedroom. Eventually I got to the age when I could join a gym. No matter where I was living at the time, I would scout out a nearby place to train, oftentimes miles away. I would ride my bike there and back. The progress wasn't what I had hoped for; neither did it have much of an effect on my social life. But the desire to be big and strong remained. I caught the bug.

Mother Nature eventually blessed me with a growth spurt, shooting me up over six feet five, and my consistent work in the weight room paid off. I introduced different combat sports and martial arts into my life. I was no longer picked on. And as my social skills also developed, I was no longer without friends.

Much has changed over the past couple of decades. But my love of the weight room, my desire to be big and strong, have not. There are many benefits to size and strength. According to the 3rd Special

Forces Group surgeon who was the first to operate on me in 2013, if I wasn't as big and strong as I was, I would be dead, giving proof to the saying that "strong people are harder to kill." Fact.

When I began my initial rehabilitation at Walter Reed following the loss of my leg, things started off slow—real slow. I lost approximately seventy pounds, I was frail and weak, but I was eager to get it all back. Even while still in inpatient status and going through three to four surgeries a week, when doctors were fighting the infection in my leg and incrementally amputating my leg higher and higher, I was training. I had the staff bring training bands and light dumbbells into my room. In between doctor visits, meals, and surgical procedures, I was training. I needed to get my size and strength back. I needed to be me again.

Now, I always knew the importance of flexibility and mobility; however, to say this was at the bottom of my priority list as a two-legged dude would be something of an understatement. I would bypass stretching regularly without giving it a second thought. And in my defense, it didn't matter. I didn't need to do it. Would it have been beneficial? I am sure the answer to that is yes. But I was able to make gains, stay relatively injury-free, and keep the time in the gym spent on things I felt were more pressing (pun intended). But during my recovery, my physical therapist, Kelly, did not allow me to skip this stuff. Instead, it was a priority.

Although a petite, kind, blonde from Virginia, Kelly was also ruthless, like Dr. Jekyll and Mr. Hyde. I am convinced that as a child she trained alongside Johnny Lawrence under sensei John Kreese and fully absorbed the motto "No Mercy" (reference The Karate Kid).

When I was in a physical therapy (PT) session, I did what Kelly told me to do. We worked on strength and endurance, but a lot of time was spent on range of motion (ROM) and flexibility. I hated it. Yes, it was painful, but that wasn't the problem. The problem was it was keeping me from clangin' and bangin'. It was time I could have been spending getting my strength back. She knew what I would rather have been doing, but she also knew how critical my ROM was going to be. She knew my goals, and she made it clear that I could spend the twenty-two hours per day outside my PT session in the gym lifting weights, but in PT, she was the boss. I put my trust in Kelly, I didn't complain, and I did the work. We both demanded it.

It probably isn't much of a surprise to know that Kelly was right. While flexibility and ROM are important for all of us, for an amputee, they are monumental. With the loss of muscle, the remaining muscle has to pick up the slack. And when bone is shattered and joints are damaged like mine were up around my hip, things tend to lock up. If your shoulder capsule, for example, is completely bound up due to an injury with limited ROM, the biggest deltoids and biceps and triceps in the world will cease to do you much good. You must be able to move to perform.

This lesson learned is something I continue to employ today. Despite the fact that I now recognize its importance—I have seen it with my own eyes—I still despise working on range of motion (ROM) and flexibility. It's boring. There are a thousand things I would rather be doing. And while doing it, the time just drags. But here's the thing: I have to do it. To be more precise, as long as I seek to remain an athlete, a Green Beret, and just mobile in general, I have to do it. What I have recognized, mostly due to my disdain for these types of "training" sessions, is if I wait to do it, it doesn't get done. So I front-load it and do it first thing in the morning. Now, this unfortunately makes it even more difficult considering that waking up at 0400 or 0430 is already a challenge within itself, and doing so to do something I dislike doesn't help matters one bit. Regardless, it needs to get done.

Would I rather sleep an extra thirty to forty-five minutes? Yes. Would I rather get to the gym thirty to forty-five minutes earlier? Absolutely. Would I rather get to work thirty to forty-five minutes ahead of everybody else and get some tasks knocked out? One hundred percent. But the work has to happen. I must sacrifice the extra sleep, the extra reps in the squat rack, the extra time working on the product. I must forgo doing the things I want to do for the things I need to do.

The importance of this cannot be overstated because at the end of the day, success comes to those who at any moment are willing to sacrifice what they are for what they may become.

On Saturday morning, "the average" are sleeping until ten or eleven when they could be working toward their goal. When the average get home from work, they crack a beer, sit on the couch, and drown themselves in cable television when they could be making strides toward their objective. When the average get hungry, they eat whatever they feel like, whatever tastes good, whatever will bring them that temporary joy when they could be making progress on their mission. Each and every one of these moments provides an opportunity to improve. But first we must be willing to make the sacrifice.

Every amputee starts out on a prosthetic with a socket. The socket is the shell or cup that the residual limb (a.k.a. "stump")[9] fits inside. The socket is held to the body by one or more mechanisms known as the "method of suspension." Prosthetists use several methods of suspension; however, for most, especially initially, it is with the use of a liner. The liner is a silicone sleeve that is rolled on over the residual limb that provides a means of protection to the skin and limb itself while it also, through the use of a pin or seal, locks into the socket.

---

9   Apparently, "stump" is an offensive term for some, so use it with caution. I will call mine what I choose.

A common practice used to fabricate the socket is the use of plaster, the same as a cast to secure a broken limb. The cast, which is formed to the dimensions and shape of the residual limb, is then used to create a "test socket." The test socket is made with plastic to allow for immediate and quick adjustments. Prosthetists are able to see through the plastic to the limb for any gaps or pressure points and then heat it up and reshape it as needed. Once the test socket is trialed and good to go, the next step for most is to fabricate a socket out of carbon fiber, a much stronger and lighter material, however, a permanent product.

Every amputee is different: our anatomy is different, our level of activity is different, our environments are different. There are many variables to consider. However, it is safe to say that most amputees have some combination of bone, muscle, and tissue within their residual limb, which again is underneath a tight-fitting, silicone-like material jammed into a socket. It is also safe to say that sweat is the archnemesis of the amputee.

As we move, particularly in warmer weather and particularly during high-energy activity, we sweat. With the residual limb buried underneath silicone, it cannot breathe. Yes, this becomes uncomfortable, and yes, this can force an amputee to occasionally or frequently take off the prosthetic, remove the liner, and wipe it down. An even greater impact, however, is the loss of volume within the residual limb itself.

While the limb is compressed and losing fluid via sweat, the tissue shrinks. Note: sweat simply speeds up the process. For many, the loss of volume can occur even with minimal activity and/or within cooler environments. This can pose some problems. The liner may become too loose for a proper fit, or the limb shrinkage may result in the inability to gain suspension with the socket. Fortunately, interventions can assist with these issues. "Socks," for example, are sleeves of soft material, like cotton, typically worn over the liner without impeding on the method of suspension so as to thicken up the residual limb to regain suspension. This is a helpful tool to have available if and when the need arises. Unfortunately, with the introduction of things like socks, you lose intimacy with the socket. A delay is created. When you move, it now takes longer for that energy to transfer to the prosthetic, since now it has to move through another conduit. You also have a more insulated feel with the ground or whatever object the prosthetic makes contact with. Interventions like socks are great in a pinch; they can artificially increase the volume of a limb so you can continue to function in the prosthetic, but what about when the limb gets bigger? Bottom line, the prosthetic will almost certainly become useless. It is quite simple to make the limb larger, but it is quite difficult (impossible really) to make it smaller.

In the early stages of use with a prosthetic, particularly if the limb was lost traumatically, there is a substantial adjustment period. The residual limb will decrease in volume drastically throughout the day as the limb heals and adjusts to its new situation. Eventually, however, it tends to level off. Amputees may always have to adjust for the loss of volume throughout the day, but it typically becomes less drastic, and once the prosthetic and liner are removed for a bit of time, the residual limb returns to its "normal" shape. In order to get into this type of rhythm, the amputee must monitor and control his body mass index. Any substantial gain or loss in mass will create a situation where the limb no longer fits within the socket, or at the very least, doesn't fit comfortably. So if a pain-free, functional life is to be lived with a prosthetic, nutrition must become a priority.

The importance of nutrition is something I have been aware of for a while. As a two-legged guy, however, I felt I could "out-train" any poor nutritional choices. It didn't really matter. If I decided to crush two large pizzas to the face one night, I could just hammer down a little harder the following day, and if I gained a pound or two anyway, it didn't matter. I didn't care. My training always prioritized performance over aesthetics. And while my training goals are still very much performance-based, the addition or subtraction of extra mass has a direct effect on my functionality, and therefore my performance.

The more I weigh, the more weight I have to move when I walk or run. This is, of course, the case for everybody; but, as an above-the-knee amputee, the challenge is amplified. And as previously mentioned, this extra weight can affect my ability to wear my prosthetic.

I have basically zero muscle in my residual limb. Afghanistan isn't exactly the cleanest place on earth, and as I waited for the MedEvac bird with multiple open wounds, my leg became a breeding ground for bacteria. Infection set in and essentially ate my quadriceps and hamstring. And while I would absolutely prefer to have these muscles available for use, the lack thereof works to my benefit: I don't have to worry about muscles growing or shrinking. I do still need to be aware of my body composition. Tissue will expand or contract with an increase or decrease in body mass.

The importance of nutrition increased tenfold once I became an amputee and recognized the significance of a consistent body mass index. The socket I wear is made of carbon fiber. It is a fixed shape. If I allow my limb to grow or shrink significantly, at best I will be left with a poorly fitting socket that decreases performance, causes chaffing or pressure, and results in discomfort or worse—a break in the skin that can lead to serious problems such as another infection. I no longer have the luxury to "out-train" poor nutritional decisions.

Every additional unnecessary pound not only increases the difficulty to move but also increases the chances of a poor prosthetic fit.

I am half Italian. I grew up eating pasta, ravioli, and lasagna. I love it. I will always love it. Nonetheless, Italian food is typically not the wisest nutritional choice. (Sorry, Grandma). I would eat pizza and spaghetti every single day if I could. But I can't. I can't afford to. Neither my profession nor my lifestyle allows it. I must sacrifice my desire to annihilate food that is not in my best interest in exchange for my health and my performance.

Sacrifice is giving up something we are fortunate to have: television, tasty food, a warm bed, fun with friends. Let's go even bigger, because through sacrifice we can gain two critical resources: time and money. Trade the car for a cheaper one. Maybe sell the car and take the bus. Donate the Xbox. Trade the house for a small apartment. No more eating out whatsoever.

Let's just examine that last one for a minute. What is to be gained by punting on going out to dinner? How much time does it take to get ready? How much time does it take to drive to and from the restaurant? How long does it take to eat? How much was the check? Quick math—I'm going to average this thing out at three hours and seventy-five bucks. Multiply that by the number of times we do this in a year. Now add the brunches, lunches, and whatever other reasons we go out to eat. How can we reinvest those resources?

Sacrifice—the act of forgoing our privileges.

Coupled with sacrifice is time management or, better put, time prioritization. Everybody has a problem with time. It is our most limited resource. I didn't have time. I ran out of time. Blah, blah,

blah. Check it out. The fact of the matter is this: We all have the same twenty-four hours in each day. The greats simply spend their twenty-four wisely. They have the discipline to pass on that night at the club, to put down their phone and spend time with their kids, to get that assignment done in advance so they can read a chapter ahead. While the average are sleeping until ten or eleven, the greats are up at five or six. While the average are lost in television, the greats are reading and studying. While the average are eating a Big Mac, the greats are eating healthy foods.

***

WATCHING FOOTBALL ON SUNDAYS has been a tradition of mine since I was a kid. I can still remember watching the Patriots with my father (getting 9.5 with the spread) on a small black-and-white television with the bunny ears antenna. I loved it. I've upgraded my television a bit since then, but my love of the game remains the same.

In July 2020, the summer of COVID-19, I decided to write Objective Secure. I knew I was going to have to prioritize my time. I was going to have to make sacrifices. Life on an ODA is busy. Early mornings, late nights, taxing actions in between, and consistent travel, often for extended periods of time with sporadic connectivity to home. It takes a toll, yet demands laser focus. As a family man on a detachment, time with my wife and sons are just that much more precious. I cherish every opportunity.

When examining "free time" in between work and family, it is amazing how little we may have. I took a close look and determined a couple of things. (1) Outside of work and family, I live a relatively dull life. I say this laughing, but it's true. I typically spend time in the gym, on the mats training Jiu Jitsu, reading, and, during the fall, watching football. (2) It was clear. Football on Sundays had to go. Doing so provided at least six additional hours per week to spend on this project. Those were six hours I needed.

At first, it was tough. On some Sundays, extended family or friends would come to the house. I'd be tucked away in our office hammering away on the keyboard with the sounds of cheering coming from the living room. Over time, it has gotten easier. I catch the highlights on the way into work in the morning. It's not the same as watching it in real time, but I am confident the sacrifice will be worth it. At the end of the day, it is a choice. And in this moment, I choose to share these lessons with you.

The greats create schedules and systems that maximize the use of their twenty-four. The greats have the discipline to squeeze every single ounce of progress out of every one of their twenty-four, because the greats are willing to make the sacrifice.

Why do we struggle with time? Why is time our go-to justification for not doing or accomplishing something? There are, of course, many reasons for this; my top three are (in no particular order):

+ **LAZINESS DUE TO A LACK OF PASSION:** In other words, we aren't pursuing a dream, or we are pursuing the wrong dream. We have no objective to secure.

+ **IMPROPER PLANNING:** Parkinson's law suggests work expands to fill the space and time available for its completion. In other words, if we were given sixty minutes to complete a task that requires only thirty minutes, we still take sixty minutes to complete it.

+ **WORKAHOLIC SYNDROME:** High performers seek to create more value with less effort, whereas workaholics seek to simply do more. High performers invest significant focus on strategy and the mental game, allowing them to exert less effort in the physical game.

Sit tight—we will address all of these and more as we progress.

So when we say "I will always place the mission first," what we are saying is, "I will make the necessary sacrifices, and I will prioritize my time."

I WILL NEVER ACCEPT DEFEAT.

THIS STATEMENT HAS a somewhat obvious meaning behind it: resolve, resiliency, and toughness. The mentality is that if you get knocked down seven times, you get up eight.

THE MILITARY ADVANCED TRAINING CENTER (MATC, pronounced "Matt-see") is an amazing indoor training facility at Walter Reed where patients conduct PT, occupational therapy, and general rehabilitation. My first time seeing it is an experience I will not soon forget.

May 2013. I was nearing the end of my inpatient status at the hospital and eager to get out of the room I had been living in for around ten weeks. It was there that I met Kelly for the first time. She walked into my room, introduced herself, and asked if I would like to check out the facility where I would be conducting my PT once in outpatient status. I, of course, said yes. She pushed me in my wheelchair across the hospital grounds for what seemed like an eternity. (Walter Reed is like a city.) Upon arrival, the very first thing I saw was a quadruple amputee wearing a harness that was suspended from the ceiling along a set of fixed rails that ran above the indoor track. Let's call him Travis. It took me a minute to comprehend what I was seeing. As if my steady dose of pain medication wasn't enough to cause confusion, witnessing a dude with no arms and legs walking seemingly effortlessly was difficult to absorb. My gaze shifted to the rest of the people in the room. There were some on treatment tables being stretched by therapists, others lifting weights, others dragging sleds, others balancing on foam pads, most of whom were missing at least one limb or were wheelchair-bound. Spouses and children were all around—some cheering on their service member; others working on school assignments. I was amazed. I attempted to soak it all in. This was going to be where I took things up a level. My excitement built. Then, boom! Travis had wiped out. He dangled from the ceiling, held by the harness and suspension line, with an enormous grin on his face. As a couple of physical therapists casually reset him to walk again, I asked Kelly, "When do we start?"

Getting into a prosthetic for the first time is another memorable experience. The prosthetic department at Walter Reed, just down the hall from the MATC, has a room designed specifically for this momentous event. It is equipped with a lane for walking between a set of parallel bars. These bars are adjustable to the height of the amputee so they may be raised or lowered to be around hand level. This gives patients something to hold onto in case they fall while attempting to walk.

I arrived first thing in the morning. My physical therapist, my father, and Toni (now my wife), were all present. My prosthetist, Art, showed me how to get the leg on. After several minutes of micro adjustments to my fit, it was time to walk. I was excited, eager, anxious, and nervous. I had been dreaming of this moment for quite some time. Getting back on two legs was a critical component to mission success. Was I ready for this? Did I have the strength? Was I about to embarrass myself in front of my family? There was only one way to find out.

Art provided minimal instruction, simply telling me that to activate the knee I needed to drive into the foot using my hip. My response was, "Roger that," although I hadn't a clue as to what that actually meant. The next thing Art said to me was, "Okay, now walk." With cameras rolling and my hands gripping the bars with all the strength I could muster, for the second time in my life, I took my first steps.

The walking path was only around twenty-five feet. Slowly, I staggered and stumbled down to the end and turned around. My loved ones had tears in their eyes, and Art was smiling. He just said, "Nice job. Now walk back." We repeated this process several times. In between each iteration, Art would adjust my prosthetic and tell me to do it again. Then again. And again. Back and forth I went, each time further loosening my grip on the bars. I was getting into a rhythm. This wasn't so hard. I got this all day. Then boom! I was on the floor, an inevitable part of the process.

My training in the MATC began gradually incorporating the use of my prosthetic, slowly increasing the duration of time the prosthetic was worn and the amount of weight put through the prosthetic. Initially, I was simultaneously using crutches to minimize the stress and to assist with balance. Eventually, I transitioned to a single crutch, then a cane. Soon I was moving out with both hands free. Zero assistive devices. It felt good.

I was in a hurry. I had things to do. I was convinced the harder I pushed, the faster I would get back to the things that were waiting for me. Part of my daily training was simply walking laps around the MATC's indoor track. Over time, my speed increased. Additionally, I would carry weight while walking laps: a rucksack,[10] dumbbells, kettle-bells, anything to increase the difficulty of the walking. At one point, I asked Kelly if she was going to attach me to the suspension rig, like I saw Travis using. Her reply was no. She said falling is inevitable and you need to learn how to fall and also how to get back up. Roger that.

The MATC is the ideal spot for distinguished visitors (DVs) to visit. It is common on any given day to see generals, professional athletes, musicians, even the president of the United States in the MATC. What I always enjoyed was their reaction when somebody fell down. Here they are shaking hands and taking photos, then crash—a double amputee just hits the deck. Of course, their immediate response is to rush over to assist. But then they look around to staff members to gauge their response. Sometimes staff members casually stroll over to the patient. Oftentimes, they do nothing—literally nothing. For one, they are used to it. This is, after all, a daily occurrence. Beyond that, learning to fall and learning to recover were essential training for us. So, barring some sort of serious situation, they were not about to hijack valuable training even when the leader of a nation was present.

On one particular day, I was walking my laps around the track. One step at a time. The MATC was packed. In fact, a bunch of New York Yankees were there visiting service members. I typically avoided these "meet and greet" moments like the plague. When in the MATC, I was working. Kelly knew this and did an amazing job of shielding me from unnecessary distractions. I'm pretty sure she literally hissed at a dude one time like an angry cat. Given that on this day it was the Yankees, I was even less interested. (Go, Sox.)

I was in a good stride. My prosthetic had a solid fit that day, and I needed to push it. I decided to hold a ninety-pound barbell straight

---

10   Military-style backpack.

overhead to increase the difficulty. Off I went. Shoulders burning, core burning, glutes burning. Perfect. We were working. I picked up speed. I didn't have a set number of laps in mind; I just planned on going until I couldn't go anymore. My body began to twitch uncontrollably. Fatigue set in. I was right at muscle failure. "I got one more lap in me. Let's go." I rounded the corner of the track and lost my balance. I already knew how this was going to play out.

My wipeout was of epic proportions. The barbell went one way, my body another, and my prosthetic detached completely. It was a total yard sale. The barbell slammed on the floor, clanging around, looking for a target. It found the legs of a physical therapist who was coaching a patient through a stationary bike workout. The therapist fell back onto the floor with a thud, knocking the wind out of her. My body went flailing into a rack of medicine balls neatly organized according to weight, the heavier ones at the bottom, the lighter ones at the top, all of which were now bouncing or rolling in all directions through the facility.

The photo op with the Yankees stopped. The stretches stopped. All conversation stopped. Everything stopped. As I lay on the ground, I conducted a quick damage assessment. Fingers, arms, leg, head—everything seemed to be functioning. The therapist I (the barbell, technically) knocked over regained her breathing ability. I asked if she was alright. She was fine and asked the same of me. I looked around the gym to see that nobody had moved an inch. Nobody, including Kelly, had made the slightest attempt to either slow me down before I wrecked, or come to my aid once I did. It was business as usual.

I strapped my leg back on and staggered over to Kelly. The only damage was to my pride. "You good?" she asked.

"Yeah, I'm good. Think I didn't swing completely through and my foot hit the ground behind me."

"Yeah, that sounds right. Now go pick up all the med balls and meet me over at the squat rack."

———

GETTING UP after getting knocked down in the literal or figurative sense is critical, but we need to take it a step further.

People tend to have a negative relationship with failure, as if failure is something that is to be avoided at all times. In actuality, failure is a good thing. It is essential. It is through failure that the successful learn, they grow, and they become stronger and better. For the greats, that's what practice is—controlled and intentional failure—because the only way to truly know our limitations is to reach the limit. We have to live at the edge of our capability.

———

I HAVE BEEN TRAINING AND COMPETING in combat sports most of my life. Wrestling, boxing, martial arts—and yes, I got in plenty of reps on the streets.[11] In basic training, I received my Level One (Beginner) certification in the Modern Army Combatives Program (MACP)—foundational hand-to-hand fighting techniques derived from Brazilian Jiu Jitsu (BJJ) and kickboxing. Upon graduation from the SFQC, I quickly attended and completed the MACP Level Two (Intermediate) and Level Three (Instructor) courses. I also attended and graduated from the Special Operations Combatives Program (SOCP) course—a program focused more on tactical hand-to-hand

---

11 I wasn't always an officer in the United States Army.

engagements that incorporates wearing full kit[12], the use of weapons, and fighting as a team. Concurrently, I decided to advance my BJJ skills and joined a local gym that taught both BJJ and mixed martial arts (MMA) to advance my craft even further.

After a few years training out of the same gym, I realized what had certainly been the case since formal BJJ and MMA gyms opened—it is a revolving door. Especially with the popularity of the Ultimate Fighting Championship (UFC), what was once a very quiet, niche sport became known in everybody's household overnight. This led to the BJJ/MMA gyms exploding with students. After all, it doesn't look all that hard on television. But just as fast as people came into the gym for their three or four free-trial classes, they were never seen again. Is this the result of the physical rigors of the sport? Sure. However, more than that is pride.

Let's face it, if you are on the ground being smothered by somebody and are helpless to do anything to stop it, it's not only scary; for many, it's traumatic. It is not a pleasant feeling. When that fight-or-flight instinct kicks in, but you are literally unable to do either, it's a bad day. And despite the coach's instruction and constant reminders that this is completely normal for new students and consistently reinforcing that it will get better, most don't return. What once seemed easy while sitting at the bar watching the professionals work, now not so much. The realizations that (1) "this is not at all easy" and (2) "I am not nearly as tough as I once thought" are too difficult to digest. The thought of going back into that environment is unbearable. Ignorance is bliss. This, of course, is accompanied by a host of justifications and/or ridicule for the sport. But the fact remains that the necessary dose of humility was too difficult to accept.

---

12 The tactical rig, worn on the torso, that houses our protective armor plates and a series of pouches to hold various essentials.

—————

OUR EGOS DO NOT DIGEST FAILURE EASILY. Our egos want us to constantly project strength, ability, and knowledge. Our egos can prevent us from asking questions and pushing our limitations. Unfortunately for the ego, however, asking questions and pushing our limitations are necessary. They are requirements and particularly necessary when seeking to overcome adversity. Accepting failure is hard enough as is; when attempting to do something rare, or something that has a low probability of success, the acceptance of failure is reduced tenfold. We are so determined to prove the naysayers wrong or so determined to prove ourselves right, the challenges seem to be amplified. Introduce *humility*—the preferred weapon of choice.

Humility requires allowing ourselves to become vulnerable, to expose our weaknesses—things that are extremely difficult for most, and for individuals who work in the special operations community, they are next to impossible.

The Special Operations Forces (SOF) community is one that projects aggressiveness, physical ability, intelligence, and capability.[13] The personnel within the SOF enterprise embody these attributes as well. We have mottos such as Sine Pari (Without Equal), RLTW (Rangers Lead The Way), the Quiet

---

13 A common, yet understandable, mistake is using the term "Special Forces" when referring to *all* elite military units or personnel in the military. Special Operations Forces or SOF is actually the correct vernacular in this context. Technically speaking, the term "Special Forces" (SF) refers specifically to the US Army Special Forces, a.k.a. the Green Berets. So the Navy SEALs, Army Rangers, Marine Raiders, Army Special Forces, etc., all fall under the umbrella term Special Operations Forces, a.k.a. SOF.

Professionals, and The Only Easy Day Was Yesterday. Our creeds are filled with similar language: "I persevere and thrive on adversity." "I will always keep myself mentally alert, physically strong, and morally straight." "If knocked down, I will get back up, every time." "I will not fail those with whom I serve."

These organizations hold their members at the highest level: to succeed at any cost, to remain strong in the face of adversity. While necessary, this makes accepting failure that much more challenging. When it comes to trying something new or something difficult, we must anticipate our sense of pride. We must know going in that our ego is going to argue against it. Preparedness is essential. For many, humility is a weapon that has been collecting dust for quite some time. Let's get into that arms room,[14] pull that sucker off the rack, dust it off, clean it, perform a functions check, and have it ready to get into the fight. So when the time comes, and we fall flat on our face, literally or figuratively, we are prepared.

It is normal to fear failure. Psychologically, we are designed to do just that. The successful, however, are the ones who are not only unafraid of failure; they seek it. They hunt it. They literally stalk it, and by doing so, are able to extract the lessons from that failure, take that wisdom, and ram it back into the system so they are able to work smarter. Failure is not the end of the game; it is the start of the next round. If failure were the end of the game, there would be no greats like Einstein, like Jordan, like Oprah, like Tony Robbins. If these people stopped at failure, the world would not be filled with

---

14 A secure facility to store weapons.

their accomplishments today. Thomas Edison didn't fail; according to him, he simply found ten thousand ways of creating a lightbulb that did not work. He needed only one way that did work. Failure is just one more way not to do something, or as Einstein said, *failure is success in progress.*

It's the same as the elephant and the rope. How many of us are going through life clinging to a belief that we cannot do something, simply because we failed at it before? Failure is a part of the journey, part of learning, part of the process. The only limitations that exist are the limitations within our mind.

So when we say, "I will never accept defeat," what we are saying is strive for failure, and when you reach it, learn from it, apply it, and keep moving forward. Or as John C. Maxwell says, "Fail early, fail often, but always fail forward."

I WILL NEVER QUIT.

INITIALLY, THIS SOUNDS SIMILAR to what we just talked about, but upon further examination, we will recognize the difference. "I will never quit," is about avoiding complacency. It is not letting ourselves get comfortable, not celebrating too long, not accepting the status quo, and not growing stagnant. It is adopting the principle that *satisfaction* doesn't exist and that now is the time to attack.

WHEN THE DECISION IS MADE to become a Green Beret, for most, at least for any who have bothered to conduct some research, it is recognized as a lofty goal. To put it another way, it is unlikely to be accomplished. It is a goal at the top of a very tall, steep, and jagged mountain. The individual can barely see it because there are so many obstacles in between the start point and that summit. He or she dreams of donning that Green Beret for the first time so clearly and so often—all the while knowing just how improbable it is.

When that person is successful, when he reaches the top of that mountain and dons that beret, I can attest to that feeling of accomplishment, standing on the parade field with friends and family in attendance. When given the cue, the graduating class dons the beret and snaps to the position of attention and salutes for the playing of the *Ballad of the Green Berets*.[15] It is a moment every Green Beret remembers. The previous eighteen to twenty-four months (on average) has consisted of sleeping in swamps, foot movements that seemed to go on forever, sleep-deprived mission planning, injuries, failures, and stress. But we made it. We did it. We are Green Berets. And here is the problem, here comes the threat: satisfaction.

Many will show up to join that team on day one still believing that they are at the top of that mountain. Becoming a Green Beret was the pinnacle, the top. They accomplish their goal, and the fire burns out. The motivation is gone. It's all downhill from there because they made it. This inaccurate perception is short-lived.

These individuals will quickly and painfully realize that they are back at the bottom of a new mountain. It is day one all over again. From this point, one of two things will happen: they will ignite a new fire driving them toward actually learning their job, or they will be unwilling to do so because they are content with simply being a Green Beret. Needless to say, these individuals do not last long and it is because they became satisfied with their success.

Ambitious goals are great. Some would ask, "If we aren't striving toward something difficult, then what's the point?" Oftentimes what seemed like the mission actually wasn't the mission at all; it was an objective. And this is fine. My mission was to become a Green Beret. To do that, I had to complete a long list of objectives along the way.

---

15 A song made famous by Sergeant Barry Sadler.

But what I realized once I got to the ODA and began my profession was that the detachment is a vehicle, a mechanism. Getting to the team began as the mission, but in actuality, the team is what allows us to execute the mission. I wanted to become a Green Beret, among other reasons, because I wanted to make as much of a difference as a single person could make. I wanted to be among the people to answer the call when a difficult problem had to be resolved. The detachment is what resolves the problem. That was the mission. To be on the detachment, you must be a Green Beret. To become a Green Beret, you must pass SFAS and the SFQC. So, as it would turn out, becoming a Green Beret was in fact an objective all along. It simply took me reaching the top of that mountain to be able to see it for what it was.

Regardless of the goal that has been met, you cannot remain stuck on it. Do you deserve a celebration? Absolutely. Pat yourself on the back, enjoy a nice meal, have a drink with your friends, but keep it short. After that you must locate the next ridgeline, because for the successful, satisfaction does not exist. They are constantly looking to improve. They are looking toward that next objective.

PATIENCE VS. PROCRASTINATION

Patience:

1. the capacity, habit, or fact of being patient
    (*Merriam-Webster*)

Procrastinate:

1. to put off intentionally and habitually
2. to put off intentionally the doing of something that should be done (*Merriam-Webster*)

Patience is a dangerous word. While necessary, this can very easily become our number one limitation. It is when patience transforms into procrastination that we have a problem.

Missions take time. Most take a long time. Malcolm Gladwell in *Outliers* tells us that it requires ten thousand hours of work on any particular craft to be in contention for greatness. To put this in perspective, if we spend twenty hours per week working on our mission, it will take us just under a decade to hit ten thousand hours. That's twenty hours in addition to all other requirements and priorities within our lives.

Gladwell's case studies present a convincing argument with regard to the ten thousand hours. I strongly recommend reading his work, but whether we must reach that exact number or not is not the point. The point is, it is going to take a while. When we make the sacrifices, when we prioritize our time, when we push to failure and get back up, it will still take a while. Without these philosophies, it simply won't happen at all. So yes, because this will not happen overnight, we must exhibit *patience*.

Patience has a remarkably close relationship with discipline, something we will hit hard here in a bit. Patience is consistency without immediate results. Patience is trusting the process. Patience is remaining focused on the task at hand, while also referencing the mission. Now let's discuss what patience *is not*.

Patience is not thinking good thoughts or praying, then waiting around for the universe or a higher power to provide things to us.

Patience is not going fifty percent today because we are three years out from reaching the goal. Patience is not stalling because it's not the right time to start. This is called procrastination.

———————

JUNE 2013. Moving into Building 62 at Walter Reed with my father was a glorious day. Building 62 is one of the primary outpatient residences for service members to live in once discharged from inpatient status. Rather than living in a hospital room, patients are moved into an apartment and simply commute to their required appointments throughout the day. This is a substantial step in the recovery process. Building 62 is freedom. No more doctors or other specialists bombing into my room throughout the day, no more hospital food, no more being woken up at all hours of the night to get my vitals checked.[16] This was my first opportunity after three months or so to live somewhat normally. My newly acquired freedom, however, was a Trojan horse—with it snuck in a challenge I was content to avoid.

I was yet to be on a prosthetic. I still had some rehabilitation to do, and my leg was not healed enough to begin the fitting process. My options for movement were either a wheelchair or crutches. Using a wheelchair is a humbling experience. For me, it was an enormous shot to my pride, so I preferred crutches whenever possible. It may sound ridiculous, but at least with crutches, I was moving myself, not using a chair. Unfortunately, at this time, I did not have the strength to go very far on crutches.

———

16   They have a job to do. I am grateful for them all, but it is damned frustrating.

Toni would visit me whenever possible. We both wanted to get off the Walter Reed installation and do things together: visit the sites in our nation's capital, go to a nice dinner, do anything, really. But I put it off. I didn't make any excuses. With her, I didn't need to. I was honest about the fact that I didn't want to go out in public in a wheelchair.

Ego, as I just discussed, absolutely played a role here—one hundred percent. I knew it then as I know it now. But what I told myself and Toni was that there was no rush to get out and do stuff. What's the rush? I am going to be here for a while; we will have plenty of time to see the sights and go to Georgetown Cupcake.[17] I thought I was being patient. What I was actually doing was procrastinating.

Procrastination for me stemmed from my pride. And that's the thing with procrastination: there is almost certainly going to be an underlying cause. We must ask ourselves why we are putting this off. Perhaps it's just a rough day, and nothing whatsoever seems appealing. Fine. But if a particular task just continues to get kicked down the road, we need to stop, assess the situation, and determine the actual problem.

Toni did what partners do best. She beefed up my confidence in a way only she was able to do, and then we cruised the National Mall. I even let her push me in my chair. How did I get so lucky?

---

17 Amazing deserts!

PERCEPTION OF TIME

Time:

1. the measured or measurable period during which an action, process, or condition exists or continues (see *duration*)
2. a nonspatial continuum that is measured in terms of events which succeed one another from past through present to future (*Merriam-Webster*)

We know that time is our most limited resource. Regardless of our age, the clock moves at the same speed. Each minute is equally valuable. Yet our perception of time can be so different during different phases of life. For this, we will use a football analogy. Football has four quarters to a game, and we have four quarters to life.

First Quarter (ages zero to twenty): We know very little. We are learning quickly, trying to figure out who we are and what life is all about. We are making mistakes—a lot of mistakes. Ideally, we are learning from each one. (a.k.a. the "clueless" quarter)

Second Quarter (ages twenty to forty): Our entire life is in front of us. We have all the time in the world to do what we want and to become who we want to be. We have it all figured out. Here is where procrastination can be misinterpreted for patience. (a.k.a. the "I have plenty of time" quarter)

Third Quarter (ages forty to sixty): We are too old to make any substantial changes. It is too risky. We are set in our ways, and we have too many obligations. Here is where we can become satisfied; whether we are happy or not, we stagnate. (a.k.a. the "it is what it is" quarter)

Fourth Quarter (ages sixty to eighty): We can do anything: take up new hobbies, start a new profession, travel the world, spend time with loved ones. A second lease on life. (a.k.a. the "enjoy my time left" quarter)

Now I am fully aware there are exceptions to these quarters. Some know as teenagers exactly who they want to become. People in their thirties are out there getting after it, driven, on the road to reaching mission success. There are fifty-year-olds right now who are formulating a brand-new plan of attack. Some take the fourth quarter beyond eighty years of age. I got it. We may find ourselves operating with the mindset of any of these quarters, regardless of our age. These are general brackets, not statistics-based scientific facts. Take it easy.

Every minute counts. We know this. Once it's gone, it's gone forever. Each is precious. Let's focus on quarters two and three.

SEPTEMBER 2012, Wardak Province, Afghanistan. Our mission support site (MSS)[18] sat around seventy-five hundred feet above sea level in the mountains. There wasn't much to it, and not many of us there. Village Stability Operations (VSO) was what it was called. A small footprint in an austere environment asked to execute an extremely challenging mission. We loved it.

We conducted a dismounted[19] infiltration (infil)[20] onto an objective to avoid a stretch of road believed to be riddled with IEDs. When conducting any dismounted movement, the only

---

18   One of several terms used to describe the location we live and work from.

19   On foot.

20   The portion of the operation where the unit moves to the objective.

equipment you have at your disposal is what you are able to carry. The rucksack is the means to carry this gear.

I was more than familiar with rucking. It had been a staple of my training throughout my military career to this point. Although I knew how much weight I could carry, and with that, how long and fast I could move depending on the terrain, what I failed to consider was the elevation. We had been in country only a couple of weeks prior to executing this operation, and I had not fully acclimated to the altitude. This error in judgment was made by several of us on the team, a lesson we learned the hard way.

Our infil went without issue. Yeah, we were sucking wind a bit, but we successfully accomplished our task. It was on our exfil, also conducted via dismount, where things became exceptionally challenging.

Our route back to our MSS was different than our infil. This is a commonly used tactic. However, our exfil route took us up approximately an additional one thousand feet in elevation. It wasn't long before we were hurting. I couldn't believe how taxing this was on me. This was the two-legged version of myself. Collegiate athlete. Spent most of my time in the gym, in the fight house, and on the track. How in the world is this stroll kicking my ass? The altitude certainly played a role. However, the increased elevation only amplified a basic truth of rucking—ounces equal pounds.

We made it back to the MSS without issue. We looked like hammered dog shit, but nothing some pop tarts and electrolytes couldn't resolve. This lesson was one we remembered. I implore you to do the same.

When determining the appropriate rucksack, we need to be thinking about the mission. We need to choose the right-sized rucksack for the job. Choose one too small and we will not be able to bring the necessary equipment. Choose one too large and we tend to fill the extra space with things we want, rather than only the things we need. Ounces equal pounds. Next thing you know, we're humping seventy pounds instead of the sixty pounds we need. At first, this may go unnoticed. But as the miles continue, the extra ten pounds take their toll. This will undoubtedly increase fatigue and reduce focus and ability, leaving us less effective when it is time to go to work.

Same as with ounces, minutes become hours. Hours become days. Days become weeks, and before you know it, a year has passed with little to show for it.

For those in quarter two, now is the time. Yes, at this stage it is easy to believe you have your entire life in front of you, and hopefully this is the case. Regardless of the time you have left on earth, every minute still has the same value. Every minute is an opportunity. If you are still finding yourself, that is alright, but do it. Get out there and try stuff. If you feel as though you have identified your mission, whether that is based solely on a dream or based on your identified talents, go. Move. Accomplishing that mission is going to take a while *with* you going after it *now*. Do you need to be patient? Again, only in the sense where you recognize this is a long road. That's it. Any interpretation of patience beyond that will likely result in procrastination.

For those in quarter three, it is not too late. Priorities are a thing. Family, job, children—I understand this. I am in the same boat. Yes, we have obligations to these aspects of life; however, beyond that, and arguably *above* that, we have an obligation to ourselves. We have a responsibility to live life to the fullest. Are there risks associated with making a change? Sure. Is it going to be difficult? Yes. But is it going to be worth it? Absolutely, whether we are successful or not. I, for one, would rather look back forty years from now (God willing) having been defeated but grateful, honored, and proud of myself for giving it a shot. For going all out, leaving no room for doubt or regret, leaving it all on the table. Success or not, I went for it. The idea of taking that same look back, wondering what would have happened if I had just tried, or realizing that I gave it less than one hundred percent, angers me just sitting here thinking about it. Negative. I cannot allow that to happen. We still have the time. Let's go for it.

Our perception of time also has a much broader meaning linked to life in general. After all, our life is predicated on the time we have living. We can eat healthy, exercise daily, and make sound choices to increase our odds of living a long life, but the fact remains that it can end at a moment's notice.

MARCH 11, 2013. Immediately after the impact to my right leg, I knew I had been hit. A 7.62 mm round (bullet) from a truck-mounted Pulemyot Kalashnikova machine gun (PKM)[21] at a range (distance) of approximately twenty feet feels like a sledgehammer. I didn't have time to immediately examine the wound and determine the severity. I had more pressing work to do.

"Get you and this Soldier behind cover and eliminate the threat." This is what training does. It conditions your mind and body to respond accordingly. My training kicked in, and I dragged myself and Private "Smith" approximately seven feet behind an armored truck. I located a rifle lying on the ground next to me, put it into action, and

---

21 A commonly used Soviet weapon system.

took a few horribly placed shots. One of my teammates eliminated the immediate threat,[22] and although we were still receiving fire from outside the camp, I was in no position to address that problem.

"Check the status of Smith." I do as I tell myself. A quick head-to-toe sweep. No massive bleeding. I yell his name. He responds. Airway looks good. I ask him if he is okay. He says yes. Respiration seems fine. Smith is in shock, but other than that he's alright.

"Check your wounds." I rip what's remaining of my pants open to expose my right leg. It doesn't look like a leg—more like something that just came out of a meat grinder.

"Apply a tourniquet." I rip one off my kit and slap it around what's left of my leg as high as possible in my groin. Secure it. Tighten it as hard as possible. Twist the windlass[23] and lock it in.

"Check for bleeding." I am still bleeding out. It is here that I notice the river of blood flowing from me to the location where I had been struck. A stream of dark red liquid, now also pooling beneath me.

"Femoral artery is cut. You might have ten minutes to live. Keep working." I grab a second tourniquet off my pistol belt. Same application process, just below the first one. I tighten it down so hard I almost pass out after locking in the windlass.

"Check for bleeding." I still see blood trickling from my thigh, although it seems to be slowing down. Either the tourniquets are working or I am almost out of blood to bleed.[24] A teammate arrives by my side. I tell him the situation, but he is able to see for himself. The look on his face says enough. I am going to die here today.

---

22 A professional way of saying he killed the guy shooting the PKM.

23 The stick that rotates, tightening the tourniquet.

24 One way or another, all wounds eventually stop bleeding.

"Stay strong. Your teammate is worried enough. He needs your help." I bury the pain. I hide it from my face. I tell him it's fine. I tell him not to worry about me. Go work on the ones you can help. I don't know how many of our guys are wounded, but I can hear the screams all around me. I know my time has come. He ignores my orders. He does as he is trained. He applies a third tourniquet and gets IV access. For a moment, it seems as though the bleeding has stopped. He is proud of his efforts, relieved it may have worked, yet is also anticipating my death all at the same time. I extend my fist for him to bump. He does. I thank him. He doesn't respond. I tell him to pass a message to Toni. He tells me he will. Then I tell him to go; he has work to do. This time he complies.

"Get some situational awareness." For the first time since being hit, I look up and around to get a handle on the situation. We are still in contact, taking heavy enemy fire from outside our camp. Teammates and some of our infantry uplift squad members are returning fire from towers and other fighting positions. Our Air Force combat controller (CCT) is controlling multiple close-air-support platforms calling in fires.[25] I hear the first of what would be many air-to-ground engagements. I call his name. He looks at me. I yell out, "Get those motherfuckers."

"I'm on it. MedEvac is en route. Hang in there, brother."

I see a bunch of teammates and Soldiers sprawled out on the ground, including some of our Afghan partners. Some look dead; others are fighting for their lives. It's chaos, but my guys are trained for this. Everybody is working with focus. Systematically. Step by step. That is what training does. I have never in my life been so proud.

"Check for bleeding." I regain focus and get back to work. Moving

---

25 Munitions fired from aircraft or artillery.

my leg under its own power is not an option. My femur is shattered. I grab my leg with my hands and lift it. The pain surges and I almost go unconscious.

"Focus. You need to see if you are still bleeding out. Suck it up, bitch." I manage to get my thigh a couple of inches off the ground. Blood is trickling but it is tough to tell from where. I am convinced the bleeding has not been completely stopped.

"Shit, how long has it been? How much more time do I have to work before I am dead? Doesn't matter. Move." I reach into my individual first aid kit (IFAK) and pull out some combat gauze. I rip it open and begin creating a power ball by wrapping it into the shape of a ball to increase its durability and density. I release the pressure of the highest tourniquet.

"This is going to hurt." I ram the power ball into my leg, reaching upward toward my hip. It hurts. I am feeling for the femoral artery. It needs direct pressure to pinch the bleeding off. The problem is the remaining blood in my system is shunting away from my extremities to protect my vital organs. My hands feel like meat mittens. Zero dexterity or fine motor skills in my fingers. The only way I can tell I am brushing past my shattered femur is the searing shock wave it sends through my body. Going unconscious seems inevitable.

"There it is." I think I feel a pulse inside my leg. No way to be sure. But the clock is ticking. Only a matter of minutes, if that, until I am completely bled out. And only a matter of seconds before I pass out. I ram the power ball down as hard as I can. The pain rips through my body, attempting to eject from my eyeballs. I feed more gauze in on top of the power ball, just as our medics taught us. I resecure the tourniquet on top of it. Tighten the strap. Twist the windlass. Lock it in. And pass out. I wake up what I think is just a few moments later. I wasn't out for long. I look at my leg and determine my work here is done. Alright, that's enough sleeping on the job. Get back to work.

"Be there for your brothers." I drag myself maybe six feet to a teammate. He has taken a round through his calf. Nothing life threatening, although certainly painful. The guys have applied some interventions already, including a tourniquet, which seems to have stopped the bleeding, but he is in severe pain. Note: Tourniquets save lives, an essential tool, but that comes with some impressive pain for the patient. I do what I can to distract him, provide him some verbal relief. My efforts create minimal effects, but it is what I feel to be the best use of whatever time I have left, which I am certain is not long. At some point I go unconscious again.

When I come to, I am being carried on a stretcher. Seems like they are preparing me for MedEvac. I am right. How long has it been? How long was I unconscious? It doesn't matter. I am still alive. Still in the fight. The bird touches down. My teammates load me on. One of them grabs my face, looks me in the eyes, and says, "I love you, brother." My heart is full. What an honor to have served with such men. What an honor to die alongside such warriors.

Many fundamental principles of biology, physiology, and medicine were disproven this day. There is more to this story that I will share at a later time. The bottom line is, according to these principles, I should be dead. Having survived this experience has provided me with many gifts; the most impactful one is my appreciation for life.

Every day is a gift when you are on borrowed time. Your perception is altered. Time is something you no longer take for granted. My family is a constant reminder of this truth. If things had gone the way they "should have," my sons would not exist. The beautiful moments I have shared with my wife would not have happened. All of that gone.

Never to have happened. And what a shame that would be. Their existence in my life reminds me that every minute counts. Every day above ground is something to be cherished, and more importantly, not to be wasted. It can all come to an end at the blink of an eye.

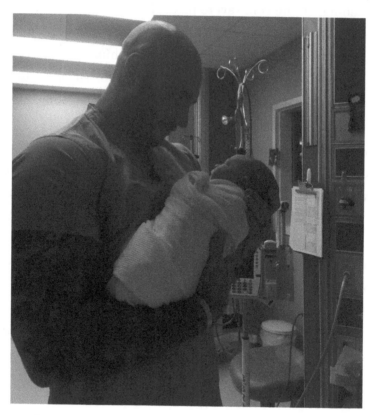

Nick and his son, Dom, Fort Campbell, KY, April 20, 2017

We cannot take our lives, our time, for granted. We must make every minute count, just like we must make every ounce count. I know in my heart it does not require coming face to face with death to achieve this perspective. It is buried within each and every one of us. For me, that's what it took. I challenge you to find it, harness it, and leverage it—without having to get your leg shot off by a machine gun.

So when we say "I will never quit," what we are saying is persist despite achievement, stay determined in the face of success, move with a sense of purpose—the time is now.

I WILL NEVER LEAVE A FALLEN COMRADE.

WE KNOW THE OBVIOUS MEANING behind this, the meaning reserved for the war fighter: the mentality that no matter what, nobody gets left behind. When we open the aperture a bit, however, this tenet is speaking to a commitment to doing whatever it takes.

Let's quickly hit some anatomy:

THE BRAIN

Brain:
1. the portion of the vertebrate central nervous system enclosed in the skull and continuous with the spinal cord through the foramen magnum that is composed of neurons and supporting and nutritive structures and that integrates sensory information from inside and outside the body in controlling autonomic function, in coordinating and

directing correlated motor responses, and in the process of learning (*Merriam-Webster*)

Our brain obviously does a lot, but sticking to the point here, it is designed, above all else one could argue, to protect us. On a genetic level, our brain wants us to avoid hazards, to avoid discomfort, to avoid stress. Our brain wants to keep us alive. Our brain has an intrinsic security system designed to keep us safe.

This system has two different alarms:

The first alarm notifies us of perceived danger or a potential threat. We know this as *fear*.

FEAR

Fear:

1. an unpleasant often strong emotion caused by anticipation or awareness of danger (*Merriam-Webster*)

———

THE COMBAT DIVER QUALIFICATION COURSE (CDQC) or "Dive School" has several tests students must successfully complete. Each is designed with a purpose according to years of data collection and lessons learned from generations of previous combat divers. The most notorious is the "one-man competency exam." During this test, students are required to wear a blacked-out mask to simulate nighttime conditions and then "surge" underwater for several currents.

Once the surge phase is complete, students are placed at the bottom of the pool and paired up with an instructor who systematically removes the students' air source (regulator) and emplaces a series of deficiencies.[26] "So how do I breathe without the regulator?" You don't. You hold your breath.

The student is required to trace the air source line from its origination point to the regulator while on a breath hold in order to retrieve the air source and breathe. This process is repeated until the exam is completed.

If this sounds awful, it is because it is just that—awful. The one-man competency exam is widely considered the most difficult test within Dive School and is the reason many do not advance in the course. There is, however, a method to this madness.

Conducting underwater operations is arguably the most dangerous task we do within the military. The ocean is unforgiving. A plethora of things can go wrong. And as with most operations, something will almost certainly go wrong. Given the fact that we as humans require oxygen above all else to live, problems underwater can quickly turn deadly.

During underwater operations, it is just you and your team. At times, perhaps, it is just you and your "dive buddy." And if things really get bad, it is just you. When a problem presents itself, you absolutely must be able to correct it. And depending on the severity of the issue, time becomes a critical factor. Every second counts. Pressure is at an all-time high. The stress of these situations can be incapacitating. The only way to work through the situation is to remain calm.

The one-man test is designed specifically to evaluate this ability prior to putting students into the ocean to begin executing dive operations. Dive School cadre (instructors) must take every action possible

---

26 In other words, problems or malfunctions that need to be corrected to regain the regulator and breathe.

to ensure students have the endurance and stress management necessary to address any potential problems that may occur, and under no circumstances freeze, or worse, leave their dive buddy due to panic.

May 2020. I was fully aware of the horrors of the one-man test prior to my arrival to Dive School. It is widely known. Dry (on land) breath-hold training is challenging, but there is no fear involved. At any point you can breathe. Once you go subsurface, things change really quickly. Removing your oxygen supply is the most unnatural thing a human being can do. For most, fear and panic begin to build within seconds. This is what the one-man test is all about. While physical ability aspects are involved, the exam predominately tests students' mental toughness—their ability to fight through natural, understandable, inevitable fear. And, as if the fear of death wasn't enough pressure, add the fear of failure, fear of embarrassment, and fear of professional consequences if dropped from the course. The stress imposed on students is monumental.

When it came time for my test, I felt confident—supremely confident. I knew I had put in the work and I was ready. While being surged, I remained calm. I thought of it more like a ride with some problem-solving mixed in. Then came the deficiency phase—although I knew going in this was going to be more difficult than my prior training, I underestimated it. As the poison that is CO_2 built up in my system as the iterations continued, my ability to focus began to deteriorate. The demons in my head screaming at me to bolt to the surface[27] were getting louder and more convincing with each passing second. I fought to remain in my "happy place." It was a back-and-forth battle.

The details of my one-man competency exam experience are unique. The lack of leg proved to be a significant challenge for this test

---

27 A major safety violation and automatic drop from the course.

specifically, one I did not account for prior to attending Dive School. Some detail into this will be disclosed here in a bit through the lens of one of my classmates, but I am proud to say that I did come out on top of that fight. Fear and I slugged it out for twelve rounds, it went to the judges, and I won by a split decision.[28] The wave of emotions after passing this assessment is powerful. For most, it is as if a twelve-hundred-pound rucksack was just dropped for the first time in weeks, proving what I had already known going in. The greatest moments in life are waiting on the far side of fear.

FEAR OF DEATH, fear of failure, fear of embarrassment—these are common and to be expected. There is, however, another fear, one that can easily be overlooked, a sneaky son of a bitch that lurks within our subconscious, waiting to come out of the shadows: our fear of success.

How can this be a fear? After all, we are striving for it, we are grinding for it, we are putting it all on the line to obtain it. True, but deep down, for many, exists the fear of making it and not being able to handle the pressure. What if I bit off more than I can chew? Am I really capable of maintaining the lifestyle once I complete the mission? Do I have what it takes to run my own company? To be a parent? To play in the NFL?

JULY 2014. Everybody was tracking (aware of) my intentions from the moment I returned to Fort Bragg from Walter Reed, to get back to the ODA.

---

28 Boxing analogy, not literal.

March 2015. After approximately eight months of advanced rehabilitation and training, I felt ready to give it a shot. I passed my first couple of physical assessments: an army physical fitness test (APFT) and a twelve-mile ruck march. I had meetings with a couple of different levels of my command that went well. Things were on track. I felt good, confident. Suddenly, what was once a pipe dream was actually looking possible.

April 2015. One night, while I was sleeping, it hit me like a punch to the gut. I popped up, heart racing, sweating. Once I figured out where I was, it set in. What if I make it back? Up until this exact moment, my desire to return to my team was about me. It was about proving wrong everyone who doubted me. "Oh, you don't think I can do it? Watch this." It was about proving the enemy wrong. "Oh, you think you took me out of the fight? You think you killed me? Well, I'm back, motherfucker." It was about proving myself right. "Nobody determines my future but me." I was fueled by anger. I was fueled by hate. I was fueled by "Fuck You." It was all about me.

As I sat there in bed, I realized something: it wasn't about me at all. I was attempting to return to a team. A team comprising ten or eleven other dudes. Dudes with families. Dudes with families every other member on the team is responsible for. What if I am successful? What if I make it back to the team and have no business being there? What if I am a liability? What if my being there puts my brothers or their families at greater risk? The questions continued to fly all night long as the doubt and the fear increased.

My ODA had just recently returned from its most recent deployment, a hard-fought six months back in Afghanistan. While my teammates were deployed, I was training. They all knew my intentions and had continuously expressed their support. But I needed to know.

After a sleepless night, I went into work and called my teammates. Most were on leave, but I was able to get ahold of the seniors. I had the same conversation with all of them. I explained where I was at in the process, although they already knew, and I explained my concern. The answer I received was uniform across the board: we want you back.

I still wasn't sure. I wanted back on the team more than anything. It was still a long shot that I would make it, but the fear of my success began to eat away at me. Were these guys biased? They are my brothers; do they just want to see me succeed out of love? Are they really thinking this through?

I continued to train throughout the week, although my focus was diminished. I grinded through my training sessions and teaching classes. My teammates on the combatives committee noticed something was up and asked several times if everything was alright. I, of course, lied and said I was fine. My next assessment was the following Monday. Was this the end of the road?

I had heard a few weeks prior that my ODA was getting a new team sergeant. This was in line with the standard team sergeant rotation, approximately every two years. What was not standard about this, however, was who was set to take the team: Master Sergeant Jimmy Rooney. Jimmy was and is a legend in 3rd Special Forces Group. He had already served his tenure as team sergeant on a previous ODA and was currently working as the noncommissioned officer in charge (NCOIC) of the Special Forces Advanced Urban Combat (SFAUC) committee responsible for teaching Green Berets and other members of the SOF community close-quarters battle (CQB) and urban combat. The SFAUC was housed in the Advanced Skills Company (ASC), same as the SOCP committee, so we all knew each other well.

The SOCP committee and the SFAUC committee worked closely together throughout the year. My SOCP teammates and I taught a block of instruction during every SFAUC class and also served as opposition force (OPFOR) during force-on-force scenarios where the situation was designed to go "hands-on."[29] I had no idea at the time, but Jimmy was watching.

It was the end of the week. Everybody had left for the day. I was lying on the couch in our office within the ASC headquarters, a place we rarely spent any time as we were typically in the fight house or on the range. I had Brazilian Jiu Jitsu (BJJ) practice to get to, but I was hurting. The soreness in my body wasn't the problem; it was my mind. I was just about out of the game mentally. Fear of success had just about knocked me out of the fight, and I was awaiting the inevitable—failing my next assessment and then going back to the drawing board of life. Enter Jimmy Rooney.

Like a message from a higher power, Jimmy leaned his head into our office, knocked on the open door, and said, "Hey, Nick, do you have a minute?" Jimmy and I had engaged in several conversations prior. In fact, it was a conversation with Jimmy that prompted my request to initiate the process to return to operational status. But we typically dealt with his instructors.

"Yeah, man, come on in," I replied as I sat up and offered him a seat.

"You alright? You haven't been yourself lately, and you look like shit."

"Yeah, man, I'm good. A bit tired, but it's no big deal."

Jimmy told me he had heard I had passed a couple of assessments and asked how I felt moving forward. "I feel good. Confident. I've been training hard, so we'll see how it goes." Jimmy saw right through me. Eventually I came clean. I expressed my concern about getting back to the ODA. I told him that I had spoken with the senior members of the team, and all emphatically stated they wanted me back, but I still

---

29   Hand-to-hand fighting.

wasn't sure. I felt they were too close to me, they cared for me too much, and it was possible their desire for my success had them blind to the reality of the situation. He understood.

"First off, I like where your head is at. What you are trying to do has never been done before, and I know you are one hundred percent focused on reaching your goal. So good on you for seeing the bigger picture. Second, I am not as close to you as the other guys, Nick. I have heard the stories of your exploits, but our direct interactions only span the past seven or eight months. As the team sergeant, the well-being of the team must be my number one concern. My primary responsibility is to do what is best for the detachment, the team members, and their families."

I knew all of this to be true, and I braced for what was coming next. I had no business being on his ODA.

You see, it's one thing to support somebody who is striving for a goal, and something completely different once that unlikely reality becomes a possible reality. It is at that turning point when fear can set in. It is only natural to cheer for our friends, our family—to support them in their efforts. We want to see them happy. We want to see them do well. It is when the goal looks possible, or probable in some cases, that the weight of reality can come crashing in. This is what happened to me with regard to myself, and I knew Jimmy was in the same boat.

"I want you on my team."

Jimmy didn't owe me a dime. I knew his obligation to the ODA ran thick through his veins. If he was saying it, he meant it. The details of this conversation are a story for another day. It was emotional, to say the least. The bottom line is this: I was back on track.

I went to BJJ practice with the energy of a seven-year-old after a three-hour nap. I was hitting all kinds of high-speed transitions and submissions. Our coach at one point told me to take it down a notch.

"The big guy is back, ladies and gentlemen," one of my SOCP team-mates yelled at one point. Jimmy got through to me. It wasn't fluff. There was no bullshit. His objective perspective was what I needed to hear. Fear suppressed. Let's go.[30]

THE WORDS OF JIMMY ROONEY

I HAVE SERVED IN THE US ARMY for twenty-five years, fourteen in the special operations community, both at the 3rd Special Forces Group (Airborne) and at USASOC. I have seen incredible men do amazing things under the most extreme circumstances, but none has impressed or inspired me as much as Nick Lavery.

I was working at the SFAUC course, and Nick was a lead instructor for the SOCP. Nick had been critically wounded in combat three separate times while operating within overwhelming kinetic environments[31] in Afghanistan, yet was trying to find his way back to an operational detachment. Although I had heard the name, and the legend preceded him, it was here I met Nick for the first time.

Nick carried himself as though he had never been injured. It wasn't something he spoke about regularly. He didn't view himself as a wounded warrior; he was simply a warrior. To Nick, he was just another one of the guys with a job to do. There wasn't anything special about him. This, however, is not the case as he is anything *but* ordinary.

---

30   Love you, brother. Thank you. For everything.

31   Active warfare including lethal force.

Nick's performance both mentally and physically was at a higher level than most healthy SOF operators I had ever known. From my perspective, it seemed the greater the challenge, the harder he pushed to overcome it. He seemed to view these obstacles as stepping stones on the path to his operational freedom.

I had already served two years as an ODA team sergeant and was assigned a second run at the same position on a different team—ODA 3126—Nick's detachment. The entire team was full of aggressive, intelligent, and experienced operators, but I knew Nick had set his sights on returning. After witnessing his dedication, drive, and work ethic, I decided I wanted Nick back on the team and was willing to fight, no matter how hard, to get him back where he belonged.

I recall when I first asked Nick what his intentions were with wanting to come back to 3126. Simply put, he was willing to do whatever it took, no matter how hard. He just wanted back in the fight.

Once I transitioned back to the ODA, the team and I were in the gym every day. It seemed as if Nick lived there. I remember seeing him pushing harder than anyone else, driven with such passion. It was unbelievable to see a one-legged man crush those of us with all our limbs. As we witnessed this tenacity, we would say to each other, "This is Nick's team, and he belongs back with us."

Our command was hesitant to allow Nick back on 3126 due to his injuries and the potential liability they might present during combat operations. I fought to give him the chance. I truly felt that although an above-the-knee amputee, Nick was a strong, competent, and valuable Green Beret—an asset we desperately wanted to employ. Our command agreed and gave Nick the opportunity to demonstrate his abilities through a variety of tests and assessments, the final one being the operational readiness test (ORT).

The ORT is an extremely difficult assessment even for able-bodied men. Some events are arguably impossible for an above-the-knee amputee—such as the depth drop. In this event, an individual must climb up a four-foot platform wearing a fifty-pound weighted vest, jump off, and make an athletic landing without touching the ground with his hands. Nick's mechanical knee was incapable of articulating in a dynamic fashion and prevented him from sticking the landing. For weeks, Nick drilled this event, starting on a one-foot platform with no additional weight and gradually increasing height and weight over time. The method he developed to complete this event was to land in a "pistol squat" position—essentially a single-leg squat landing. The guys and I watched him practice this over and over again. The mere thought of doing this myself made my knees and hips hurt, but Nick insisted it was possible. He meticulously measured out the distance from the platform to where his heel needed to land, marking it with tape on the ground. Too far forward and he would fall backward upon landing; too close to the platform and his knee may explode. He approached this event like a science experiment, a problem that needed to be solved through trial, error, and work.

On the day of Nick's final physical assessment, the ORT, it felt as if the entire unit was present. Nick was attempting to make history as the first above-the-knee amputee to return, not just to an ODA but to an ODA set to once again deploy to Afghanistan to conduct combat operations. Everybody was in awe watching him perform. When he completed the last event with our entire command in attendance, he was given approval to return to the team. It was one of the most memorable moments we shared.

So how did Nick put his mind and body in such a positive, motivated, and influential place to become so well-known as not only one of the most aggressive warriors but also a life coach, teacher, and mentor?

I believe that Nick's outlook on his environment is where it started. He had to determine what it was that he wanted in life and set a plan to achieve it. Nick could have easily become negative and bitter and could have medically retired out of the military. Nobody would have thought less of him for doing so; he had been through a lot. Instead, Nick *chose* to pursue what he identified as his *purpose*. I feel the key to Nick's success is that he clearly stated his intent and it gave him a reason to get out of bed every morning. This only grew as he continued achieving goals along the way, and Nick may not realize it, but he became a model for success in every aspect of being a phenomenal Green Beret and leader.

His sphere of positive influence encapsulates everybody he comes in contact with. Complaining around Nick is impossible. Giving anything less than one hundred percent around Nick is not an option. His actions raise the bar for the rest of us to match. His presence makes us better.

What did Nick do to get to where he is today?

Plain and simple, Nick embodies intestinal fortitude and cares about the men and the mission. Lots of people say they do, but for most, these are just words because they haven't experienced the hardships, trauma, loss, and struggles that Nick has. Nick has been in the most extreme, violent, and ambiguous combat environments and not only survived but came back stronger than before. He pushed, persevered, and refused to live a life of settling—this has always impressed me. I never saw Nick falter or fail at anything. I saw him calm during chaotic situations on the battlefield; he was all about taking care of business and performing at the pinnacle of his abilities.

Nick has earned a legendary reputation. He is a family man people can trust and confide in—he has a genuine heart and it shows. But on the flip side, he is an aggressive tactician and shooter. He is a warrior, and an overall model Green Beret. This is what he does on a daily basis. This is who Nick is.

I am honored and humbled to call Nick a teammate and a friend. He taught me how to be an effective leader and Green Beret. He showed all of us, through his actions, not his words, what is possible with a strong mind and body. Thank you, brother. Victory or Valhalla.

MSG Jimmy Rooney
US Army Special Forces

THE BRAIN'S SECOND ALARM to keep us safe notifies us of damage or impairment. We know this as *pain*.

PAIN

Pain:

1. a localized or generalized unpleasant bodily sensation or complex of sensations that causes mild to severe physical discomfort and emotional distress and typically results from bodily disorder (*Merriam-Webster*)

PRIOR TO MY ARRIVAL at Special Forces Assessment and Selection (SFAS), I had done a fair amount of research on the keys to success. A lot of the focus in what I found was relatively obvious: physical training, land navigation, leadership, etc. But there was also a fair amount of emphasis placed on your feet and keeping your feet in good condition, also known as "foot hygiene." At the time it made sense, but I really didn't give it a ton of attention. In retrospect, I should have prioritized it more.

With or without any research at all, it is safe to assume that you will spend a lot of time moving on your feet during SFAS. A quick Google search will also inform you that much of this time moving on your feet will be done with a rucksack on your back. Spoiler alert: your feet will take an absolute beating.

March 2008. It was somewhere around the halfway point of SFAS that I began letting my attention on my feet slip. As fatigue and hunger set in, I would often skip foot hygiene in order to eat and sleep as soon as possible. Not only was this dumb, it quickly spiraled into a problem. The blisters that had developed on both pinky toes were severe. We were told from day one and throughout training not to hide injuries. The SFAS cadre take this very seriously. Although it does not feel this way at the time, their number one priority, above all else, is our safety. I notified one of the cadre that I had some nasty blistering going on. He brought me to a medic to check them out. His first question was, "Have you been keeping up with your foot hygiene?" I was honest and told him that I had neglected it the past couple of days, to which he simply replied, "Yeah, you have." I had serious concerns about being medically dropped from the course. He cleaned the area, popped the blisters, applied some bacitracin, and wrapped them up. He told me he did not feel they were infected—not yet anyway. If they were or became infected, I would likely need to withdraw from training and could return to a future class.

On one hand, I was relieved that I was not being dropped. On the other hand, I knew I was walking a tightrope. He gave me some gauze, tape, and bacitracin to take with me with instructions on how to treat myself. He also said that if my feet got any worse, I needed to report to him immediately for a checkup. I agreed, thanked him, and returned to training.

I followed his guidance. Unfortunately, the problem persisted and the pain began to increase. I monitored the situation closely. I was confident that any follow-up with the medic would result in me going home. And while I was equally confident that I would get the opportunity to return, I needed to finish what I started.

Every step I took was painful. If we had been authorized to wear a pedometer or any sort of activity tracker, it would have read something like "Cannot compute total step count. See your medical provider immediately." I did not feel I was in any real medical danger. Swelling? Yes. Redness? Yes. Pain? Absolutely. But I didn't have a fever,[32] which I decided was my limit of advance. I told myself, as flawed as this may have been, that as long as I didn't spike a fever, I was okay and it was only pain.

The pain continued to increase throughout training. But I was approaching the end of SFAS. The final event was a long-distance ruck march. The distance was unknown. Candidates are simply told to move along the route. At this point, every candidate is trashed, exhausted, beat up, has decreased focus and cognitive function, and is just trying to survive. I was no different.

I treated my feet as I had been doing in preparation for this final task. I doubled up on my treatment interventions, telling myself that would take the edge off. Turned out that was a lie. Somewhere around mile four, my feet were throbbing. My brain was literally screaming at me to stop, and in my psychologically and physically weakened condition, it was remarkably convincing.

32 An indicator that an infection is becoming serious.

Mile after mile, with literally every single step, I was in a fight with myself. I could at any point simply stop, sit along the side of the road, and activate my safety strobe light, and I would be picked up by cadre and taken back to camp. "Could I do that and still be selected?" I asked myself. I did not know. And that unknown was a risk I was not willing to take. I had come too far. One of two things was going to happen. I was going to make it to the finish line or be ordered to stop. That was it. I had made up my mind.

I knew the pain was not going to end. So my next course of action was to simply finish as fast as possible. I took off running. Surprisingly, the pain did not increase; in fact I felt it decrease even just a bit. This gave me new hope. I began moving out even faster. One foot in front of the other. Keep going.

I arrived to the finish point, checked in with the cadre, and confirmed the weight in my ruck as usual. I was told to take all instructions from the whiteboard.[33] Candidates were required to check it periodically twenty-four seven for guidance. It simply read, "Shower shoes authorized to be worn on camp. Walking authorized. Shower, eat, and sleep." Possibly the greatest words I have ever read in my entire life.

After "two weeks in hell," according to the Discovery Channel's documentary,[34] I did it. I was done. I didn't make it to the shower. Instead, I proceeded to annihilate a meal ready to eat (MRE),[35] lathered

---

33 During my SFAS class, as during many prior, all timelines and instructions were written on a massive whiteboard that stood in the middle of our camp—a tradition no longer in use.

34 Worth watching, and for a real laugh check out comedian Bill Burr's rendition.

35 Self-contained individual rations for service members' use in combat or field conditions.

my mangled feet in antibiotic ointment, and crawled into the rack. I was supremely confident I had performed in a manner worthy of being selected. More than that, however, I was proud. Who knew an Army cot could be so comfortable?

The following morning, I hobbled to the medical station along with around forty other candidates to get seen by the doctor. He looked at my feet, particularly my toes, and told me I was real close to a serious infection. I knew this to be true. He gave me some antibiotics and told me to follow up with my primary care doctor upon return to Fort Bragg. I candidly asked him, "Hey, doc, if I had brought this to your attention yesterday before our final event, would you have allowed me to participate?"

He paused before responding. "I do not think you have a serious medical condition. Ten days of antibiotics and some normal activity and you will be fine, but I would have been required to hold you from training any further." He knew that I knew that was the case. "Congratulations, candidate."

OUR BRAIN AT TIMES IS A BARRIER, something we must get past. Fear and pain are convincing alerts. The ultimate salesmen who typically close ninety-ninety times out of one hundred are good. Real good. Able to "sell a ketchup popsicle to a woman in white gloves" good (*Tommy Boy*).[36] We tend to buy what fear and pain are selling, and at times it's in our best interests to make the transaction. After all, we want to be aggressive and ambitious, not reckless. But to constantly, time and time again, err on the side of caution will not

---

36 Classic comedy film starring Chris Farley.

result in success. Striving for excellence requires risk, something our brain is usually against.

THE HEART

Heart:

1. a hollow muscular organ of vertebrae animals that by its rhythmic contraction acts as a force pump maintaining the circulation of the blood
2. the emotional or moral nature as distinguished from the intellectual nature
3. one's innermost character, feelings, or inclinations (*Merriam-Webster*)

Our heart, on the other hand, both literally and figuratively, is what drives us. It's the source of our strength and the propellant for our energy. Our heart recognizes opportunity. It seeks advancement. It desires achievement. Our heart is bound by nothing, knows no limitations, doesn't consider obstacles, and is the housing unit of our greatness.

ONE OF THE REQUIREMENTS to graduate from Dive School is making a three-kilometer surface swim within a certain time standard. As part of my training, I conducted a variety of surface swims at different distances. The three-kilometer swim is one of many prerequisite events one must pass in order to attend Dive School. I was prepared for it. I was ready, and then the wheels fell off—or, in this case, my leg.

The socket I had at the start of Dive School was not a great fit. I had had it only a few weeks prior to departing for Key West. My prosthetist and I were rushed. We did the best we could. Unfortunately, it just wasn't an ideal situation, but it didn't matter. I was going to make it work.

Unlike during my previously executed three-kilometer swims, immediately prior to conducting this event during Dive School our class was provided some "remedial training."[37] Once the training was complete, we made our way to the boats. It was on the walk over I realized my prosthetic was feeling loose. Option one: notify the cadre (instructor) and, if allowed, take off all my gear, take off the leg, wipe it down, adjust it, strap it back on, get my gear back on, all while everybody waited for me. Option two: fuck it. I went with option two.

We loaded up the boats and headed out to the drop point. For this event, each student is attached to a line of nylon webbing that is fixed to a bright red buoy. This is not a personal floatation device; it is an easily identifiable object allowing the cadre to identify each student's location as a safety precaution.

On command, every student entered the water. Once giving the "okay" signal to the cadre, we were free to begin our movement and the clock started. I got my bearing, identified my reference point, and moved out. In the beginning, it's a bit of a mess. The three-kilometer swim is early in the course, so the majority of students remained. Around thirty of us were all fighting for position, getting tangled in each other's buoy lines, and of course we all wanted to win. It wasn't long until this was no longer a problem for me.

---

37 A nice way to say physical training due to making an error, a.k.a. smoke session.

As badly as I wanted to come in first, I knew this was unlikely. The prosthetic fin attachment I had at this point, although it provided a little propulsion, served more as a rudder than anything else. What was dubbed my "Finding Nemo fin" helped keep me moving straight. My sound leg was my motor. But that was okay. I had executed this task many times before. Even as the pack of students gradually gained a lead on me, I had this event in the bag.

I was around one kilometer into the event, and I could feel my socket shaking loose. Not a big deal. I was still able to get use out of it and just kept going. Then I got hit with a decent-sized wave. All of a sudden, I could move my right leg (prosthetic side). I looked under the water, and the nylon webbing connecting my buoy to me was wrapped around my prosthetic fin. As I attempted to untangle myself with the waves crashing on my head, I seemed to only be making it worse. Frustration set in, and I jerked my leg hard to free it. Not smart.

As part of my method of suspension, I have a belt connected to the socket that wraps around my waist. When I jerked my leg to get free from the buoy line, the belt ripped, and my socket came clean off my leg. Frantically, I grabbed it before it became the property of Poseidon. Now I had some problems to solve. Option one: signal the cadre on the nearest boat to come scoop me up, ask permission to reattach my leg and hopefully get approval to do so, then continue. Option two: fuck it. I went with option two.

Getting the socket back onto my actual leg was not an option while in the ocean. The best I could come up with was simply to re-rig the belt so it remained attached around my waist. The propulsion and rudder control from my prosthetic were now gone; instead it was essentially an anchor attached to my waist. If I was going to do this, it was going to be truly single-legged with a bucket trying to pull me to the ocean floor.

This was supposed to be one of the easier events for me during Dive School—one I knew was coming, one I was prepared for. Now I found myself trying to figure out just how in the hell I was going to do this. This was a short analytical process. There wasn't much to it. Just keep going.

Around the two-kilometer point, I could see only a handful of other buoys around me. I glanced behind me to see one of the safety boats no more than twenty-five meters away. This informed me that (1) I was at the back of the pack, as if I didn't know this already, and (2) there were some concerns for my well-being. The cadre were not aware of my situation. My assumption was if they were, they would have pulled me from the event for safety reasons. As I continued moving, I began to cramp. My hip, my hamstring, my triceps, and my pectorals were all beginning to cramp. I had to utilize my upper body to make up for the loss of propulsion. Finning is typically a lower-body function. My upper-body muscles were not accustomed to this much strain during this type of movement.

As I continued, the cramping increased. I was zigzagging rather than moving straight. The lack of rudder, the fatigue, made navigation a challenge. With around seven hundred and fifty meters to go, one of the safety boats pulled up alongside me. One of the cadre asked if I was alright. Clearly, I wasn't looking good. "Roger that, dive supp," I shouted back. I was obviously not very convincing, considering he responded with, "Are you sure?" It was here I quickly assessed my situation. I had no idea what my time looked like. I couldn't see any other buoys in the water. I was pretty certain I was the last student still in the ocean. Most of my body was cramping and getting worse with every passing minute. Did I even have a chance to pass this thing? Did I even have enough in the tank to finish? Was I in actual danger? The last question was what I focused on; the others didn't matter.

A key to success during Dive School and the training prior is trust, knowing with every ounce of your being that the guys around you, the dive supervisors, the safety swimmers, and the dive medical technicians (DMTs) will not let anything happen to you. If you go unconscious under water, they will get you to the surface and bring you back. You have to accept this. So that is what I did in this moment. I looked back to the cadre, and again I said I was good to go. What I said in my mind was, "I know you won't let me die here today." Everything around me was telling me to stop. My brain was screaming at me to get on the *boat. My heart, however, needed to finish.*

The last five hundred meters of this event was brutal. At times it felt like I was moving backward, like the Atlantic was taking me out to sea. Everything hurt, including my pride. I was confident I would not make the time standard and subsequently I would be forced to return to Fort Campbell a failure. When I reached the finish point, a cadre member marked me down on a clipboard, and as I lay there on the shoreline looking up at him, he just said, "You're good to go," meaning I had passed.

Combat Diver Qualification Course, Key West, FL, June 2020

THE WORDS OF "JOHN"

THE TROOP BAY PULSED with anticipation as twenty-three Air Force CCT and special tactics officer trainees received the notification that we were headed to one of the most rigorous schools in the Army: The Combat Diver Qualification Course (CDQC) also known as "Dive School." During our two-year training pipeline, we are required to learn underwater operations, rescue procedures, subsurface navigation, and stealth infiltration techniques in order to become combat divers.

Water is the ultimate equalizer. Something so inherent as the need to breathe reduces humans to the most primitive version of themselves. Their brain, their instincts, their body shifts into overdrive with a singular goal in focus: survival. The test of people in such extreme conditions lays bare their true mental fortitude and ability to navigate the most stressful of situations. That is what we were facing, and that is what we were determined to conquer.

Twenty-four hours later, my team drove the length of Florida to the southernmost part of the state. Fleming Key is an ordinary island just north of Key West. There is nothing remarkable about this patch of sand and soil until the northernmost section becomes visible. When we were driving through the gate to the Special Forces Underwater Operations compound, we could see the imposing dive tower looming over the pool against the backdrop of the ocean. Its ominous presence is a silent challenge to all who arrive with the intention of earning the coveted Special Operations Diver Badge.

For some of us Air Force trainees, this would be our first joint interaction. The Green Berets is one of the most respected special operation entities in the military, and I was looking forward to training with and learning from our counterparts. The first formation at the schoolhouse was held the following morning, and immediately everyone's eyes were on the largest man present, arguably the most enormous man many of us had ever seen. He was the type of big that is so big you notice his sheer magnitude before you notice his prosthetic. The longer I looked at him, the more I began to wonder if he was even human. The tattoos, his big, unblinking eyes, and the bionic-looking leg seemed like exactly what the military would design as the ultimate weapon. It quickly circulated that his name was Nick Lavery, a warrant officer with the 5th Special Forces Group. Many Google searches ensued, and we devoured the stories of his unparalleled courage and sacrifice. His dedication to lead and serve his teams hallmarked his selflessness. I was ecstatic to be in the company of such a man, and over the course of the next six weeks, I continued to learn what a distinct privilege it was to get to know such an extraordinary person.

Chief Lavery is a damn warrior in every aspect of the word. He is not only the embodiment of toughness and mental tenacity; he is also the whole picture of character. After training side by side with him in a uniquely demanding environment, I am convinced that three primary characteristics make Chief Lavery an undefeated gladiator regardless of the arena he is in. What I have observed and learned is an honor to pass on to you now.

When difficult circumstances arise, a critical characteristic that separates the champions from the participants is grit. Angela Duckworth, the author of *Grit*, characterizes it as "a combination of passion and perseverance" with the objective of reaching long-term goals. I interpret this as a wholehearted commitment to the grind. Chief is all in. It doesn't matter what kind of work it is, he will pay his dues and more. Regardless of the situation, he will give whatever task all he has. Before the course officially started, the class was brought to the pool as Chief and his dive buddy solved the logistics of entering and exiting the water quickly with a prosthetic, an unprec- edented situation for which nobody, including the instructors, knew the correct procedure. It was a problem that needed solving.

Initially, Chief had a very small fin (next to him, it barely existed), black in color, and with a connection at the top to lock into his pros- thetic socket. Watching Chief maneuver in the water was difficult, because he was being asked to accomplish an objective with substandard equipment. The struggle was evident, but the warrior mindset isn't dependent on ideal conditions; you don't always get the right equipment, but you must execute the mission anyway. This fin was clearly subpar. It did not allow him to generate enough power to propel him forward; neither did it create enough balance to counteract the oceanic current his other leg was producing. I am convinced this would have been a crutch for many people. The disadvantage was severe.

Grit, though, allows you to persevere even in the face of handicaps and setbacks. He made jokes about being a real-life Nemo, swimming, training, and testing with a gimpy fin. He continued to press and seized the opportunity he had been granted to attend Dive School. About halfway through the course, after we had passed the most grueling challenges, another prosthetics team was able to bring him an attachment that was not only an actual fin but also looked lethal. When Chief got in the water with his new upgrade, he was traveling with dexterity at terrifying speeds. I wouldn't be surprised if he gets his own feature during *Shark Week*.

This is the moral in his application of grit. It does not matter the circumstances—to have the warrior mindset, you grind it out. You continuously apply yourself regardless of if you feel motivated, have fair weather, or have the right equipment. You find a way. When you keep showing up, day after day after day, your preparation will meet opportunity, and when it does, make sure you are ready.

Humility is an integral facet to Chief's character. He recognizes his accomplishments, but at the core of his motivation is the desire to inspire others. Everything I learned about his achievements and awards I learned from someone or something other than Chief himself. A long line of service members came before Chief. His respect for those who preceded him is evident in how he studies and embodies the warrior ethos. He is also keenly aware of the long line of warriors who will come after him. The choice to push himself to new limits is an effort to inspire and positively impact those who will come after him. Accolades and sycophantic praise do not fuel a warrior. Like a leopard, strong, deadly, and ready to attack, silently prowling the jungle floor, a warrior can exist in the shadows without a soul knowing his name. Chief Lavery has been the first to do many things in his lifetime. During the time I trained with him, he became the first amputee to earn the prestigious qualification of combat diver. Without fanfare or celebration of this monumental milestone, Chief went back to his unit to start preparing for his upcoming deployment.

When a person is humble, it allows him to stay grounded, remembering that at one point he was a beginner. One weekend, I asked Chief about the firefights he had been in. He said he remembered his first one vividly, and the adrenaline rush was incomparable to anything else. He said he was lucky to have a senior member on the team guide him. He pointed out to Chief where the best vantage points were, where the bulk of the fire was coming from, keeping situational awareness of their team and who required immediate attention. He said, as with anything, a person becomes more proficient under fire with practice. As he became better, he was humble enough to look at the new guys and know that they would need some counsel too. He did not balk at their clumsiness. Instead, he used these moments as opportunities to invest in the next generation of warriors. Warriors remember their novice years and know that it is important to help those around them, to benefit the team or organization.

Finally, Chief's defining characteristic: resiliency. The reverence for Dive School in part comes from the one-man competency test, a grueling assessment that requires a person to perform certain tasks with limited breath under the water. Students are granted one practice attempt preceding the graded event and a retest the following day if they are unsuccessful. During the preliminary round, Chief's body used up all its oxygen too soon, causing him to black out. Because he can use only one leg, balancing while sitting on the bottom of the pool requires more effort from him. Oxygen is more precious than gold when holding the breath, and to conserve as much of it as possible, limited movement and flexion is essential for success. Chief did not have the liberty to simply relax under water. He had to continuously engage his core to counteract the movement of his arms and keep him sitting upright. His first test ended with the same result; he had passed out after an exorbitant effort to stay conscious under the surface. The next twenty-four hours were particularly tense thinking about the final attempt, because what was Chief to do? He was no quitter; he went until his body could not go any further. Two failed tests can shake a person's confidence, but the real test is how you handle that. Chief's third go at the one-man competency exam ended with success. After he exited the pool, he looked at the group waiting for him, gave us a single nod, and moved on to the next phase of training.

Over the course of those six weeks, at one of the most challenging and prestigious courses the special operations community has to offer, Chief Lavery invoked grit, embodied humility, and taught me what it means to be truly resilient. Our greatest adversary will always be life itself. No one makes it to the other side unscathed. We will suffer broken bodies, broken hearts, broken spirits from chasing a better version of ourselves; or worse, we will suffer the mundane monotony of having tried nothing and done nothing at all. It is impossible to chart your life and make it from point A to point B without detours and road closures. Chief taught me that warriors are warriors not because they can handily defeat any adversity, but because they can face it, work with it, and mold it into something new. I believe that the fuel that drives Chief's ability to rise to any challenge is his desire to show others that they too can rise, they too can conquer, and they too can be the ultimate warrior.

"John Doe"
US Air Force

WE NEED BOTH THE HEART AND THE BRAIN—both have an essential role—but when it comes to striving for success, there will come a time when we have to ignore our brain. We have to ignore that fear, push through the pain, make the hard decision, and listen to what our heart is telling us. We gotta take a shot. We have to be willing to take the risk. We have to get out of our comfort zone and be willing to fail.

DECISION POINTS

Decision point:

1. the point in space and time where the commander or staff anticipates making a decision concerning a specific friendly course of action. A decision point is usually associated with a specific target area of interest, and is located in time and space to permit the commander sufficient lead time to engage the adversary in the target area of interest. Decision points may also be associated with the friendly force and the status of ongoing operations. (See also *course of actions, decision support template, target area of interest.*) (Army Field Manual 6-0)

Everybody hits a crossroad—a decision point—the point where things get hard, and in that moment, we can either continue on track or divert, a.k.a. quit. At times, we can anticipate a decision point, perhaps not down to the exact moment, but we know it is coming.

———

THE UNITED STATES ARMY has seventeen branches with warrant officer positions. The US Army's Warrant Officer Candidate School (WOCS) is taught at Fort Rucker, Alabama. Following WOCS, candidates attend the Warrant Officer Basic Course (WOBC) at their respective branch to study advanced subjects in their technical area before moving on to their assignment as a warrant officer. Of the seventeen branches with warrants, sixteen follow this process. SF warrant officers do not.

Special Forces warrant officer candidates attend the Special Forces Warrant Officer Technical and Tactical Certification (SFWOTTC) course at Fort Bragg, North Carolina, which includes both WOCS and WOBC and is tailored to the unique training, experience, and requirements of the SF.

One of the requirements to become a warrant officer in the US Army is passing a timed twelve-mile ruck march. Rather than executing this task along a road as an independent event, the SFWOTTC course (let's simply call it the warrant course) incorporates this ruck as part of the culmination exercise (CULEX) at the end of the course. The movement is part of the infiltration into a week-long scenario designed to test candidates' ability to make decisions and perform technical and tactical tasks as a team. The ruck itself is conducted through the challenging terrain of Uwharrie National Forest in North Carolina.

I knew going into the warrant course that this event was waiting for me at the end. I had done dismounted movements in the past as an amputee, some through challenging terrain; however, I was confident this would be among the more difficult terrains I had attempted.

In January 2019, I began the warrant course. The curriculum is approximately five months long, so I had time prior to the CULEX to train on my rucking. I incorporated exercises and training methods during my daily physical training to strengthen my rucking abilities. I did extra work specific to this in the evenings and on the weekends. When it came time to perform, I felt as ready as I would ever be.

I anticipated at least one decision point. I was expecting to hit a point where I questioned my ability or desire to continue. Knowing this was inevitable allowed me to prepare. I knew my teammates would be with me. I knew the cadre had safety precautions in place; therefore, I knew I had nothing to fear. In the worst case, I would collapse from exhaustion or injure myself falling down a hill, but the guys would be there to get me out. Through this analysis, I was able to establish a contract with myself, a constitution. (1) I would put in the work now to increase the range (distance) to the decision point and (2) under no circumstances would I quit. I had come too far. This would be the last significant challenge I would face. It was the last thing standing between me and the graduation stage. I was ready for the decision point. In fact, I couldn't wait to get there.

Sure enough, I was right. Somewhere around mile eight my prosthetic began acting up. My guess was I broke it during one of the several falls I had taken prior to that point. It just wasn't operating properly. Walking became a real struggle. Our lane walker[38] ordered

---

38   A cadre member assigned to move with the team to evaluate and, if necessary, to step in to address any issues.

us to stop for a short rest. He asked me what was going on and I explained that I thought my leg was slightly broken. Unfortunately, a backup leg was not something I had decided to carry with me, but rather I had had it sent to our final destination along with the remainder of our gear.[39] He asked if I thought I could continue, to which I stated I would be fine; however, my concern was failing to make our hit time.[40] The parameters of this phase of our infil were that any team that did not make it to the end point within the allotted time would have to walk an additional four miles. Up to that point, we were making good time; however, I knew that with my prosthetic in the condition it was in, I would not be able to move as fast. As a result, the entire team would have to slow down as we were required to move as a single unit. I did not *want my teammates to suffer due to my inability to move out.*

Our lane walker understood and called the CULEX primary instructor (PI) to explain the situation. My desire to continue, along with my concerns for the team, were relayed and I was put on the phone. It was explained to me that I did not need to continue. Our PI had concerns that if I were to do so, especially on a malfunctioning prosthetic, I would be at a high risk for injury. He assured me that I would not be dropped from the course. I believed he was telling me the truth, but I could not comply. I stated that I must continue. I did not have a choice. I had to finish. I emphasized my discontent with my teammates required to ruck more than necessary at my expense and requested permission to do the additional four miles on my own.

My teammates were all standing within earshot of me during this conversation. One of them, a beast from Tenth Special Forces Group,

39 This was a stupid mistake.

40 The dictated arrival time to a destination.

also named Nick, approached to tell me that he and the guys had no issue walking the additional distance. If I wanted to continue, they were cool with it.[41] I looked to the others, and one of them said, "Gold jacket, green jacket, who gives a shit?" A perfectly placed quote from the movie *Happy Gilmore*. Everybody started laughing hysterically, including myself and our lane walker. I actually forgot I was on the phone with our PI.

I placed the phone back to my ear and said, "Chief, we are going to push on." He was also chuckling as he too had heard the Adam Sandler quote. He said "Alright" and I hung up. We pressed on.

With just a couple of miles to go, I looked up and saw our PI making his way toward us down the trail. We had already busted our time and we were all prepared to walk a little farther than originally expected. At times I felt terrible about it, and I even hated myself for forcing the extra suffering onto my boys. It was hard, however, to focus on this given the banter we were exchanging while we walked. War stories, stories about our kids, absurd and, of course, hilarious tales about experiences overseas. We were laughing our way through the mountains. In fact, it became difficult to notice just how much pain I was in. Our PI walked straight to me and asked how I was doing. There were obviously increased concerns with me doing this move- ment to begin with. I imagine there was established abort criteria built into the event's risk management for me personally. In their defense, we were traversing some gnarly terrain. I explained I was good to go, but he didn't buy it. "How's the prosthetic?"

"It's fucked," I said, "but I can make it work." Again, he explained that I did not need to proceed. He said that just another one hundred

---

41 The privilege to live among such lions is the number one thing I will miss once my days as a Green Beret are over.

meters ahead was a vehicle trail and the truck he had driven in on. I could get in it and meet the rest of the team at the end point. He said neither them nor I would be in jeopardy of a negative evaluation. He said I had proven enough, and he essentially begged me to quit.

Was my ego a factor? Probably. Am I a glutton for punishment? Maybe. Did I miss an opportunity to end the misery? Yes. So why, you ask? I knew dealing with the pain would pale in comparison to the feeling of giving up on myself, giving up on my team, quitting. My contract didn't allow it. *"Pain is temporary. It may last a minute, or an hour, or a day, or even a year. But eventually it will subside and something else will take its place. If I quit, however, it will last forever."* — Lance Armstrong.

I told the PI I wanted to press on. If he was ordering me to stop, I would, of course, do as I was told. But I felt alright, I was making it work, and the guys and I were prepared to walk the extra distance. He looked at the ground and just shook his head before looking up at me with a grin. "Alright, Mr. Lavery, you can continue if you choose. You guys have about two miles left."

This meant (1) I could finish what I had started and, more importantly, (2) we did not need to walk the extra four miles. The good news excelled our rate of speed. We plowed up and down the rest of the route with what seemed like ease. We got to the end point and were shortly thereafter picked up by a van to bring us to our MSS. We made it. All of us, together.

Special Forces Warrant Officer Technical and Tactical Certification Course graduation, Fort Bragg, NC, May 22, 2019

DECISION POINTS can also present themselves without notice and oftentimes surprisingly. These decision points are clearly more difficult to deal with—the decision points that just spring up out of nowhere.

WHILE AT WALTER REED, I was approached by a member of the Achilles Freedom Team, an organization that facilitates wounded veterans' participation in races, particularly marathons. At the time, I was willing to try just about anything that I felt would increase my physical capabilities, so I agreed to participate.

I did a few shorter race events with a provided hand-cranked wheelchair, a.k.a. a hand cycle. It took a minute to figure out how to operate this contraption, but I began to really enjoy it. Prior to this, I had not yet been able to "move out" (move quickly) under my own power, as running was not yet an option. I felt like Ricky Bobby in *Talladega Nights*. "I'm going fast again!!"

In the fall of 2013, I agreed to race in the Chicago Marathon with Achilles. It was a blast. Streets lined with people, all extremely patriotic. But more impactful than anything was it being my first opportunity to compete again since losing my leg. Competition breeds results, and it had been a while since I felt that against somebody other than myself. I enjoyed it so much I agreed to do the Detroit Marathon just a few weeks later. It was here that I found myself at a decision point I was not expecting whatsoever.

It was October. Not exactly warm. I was grossly underprepared. A stretch of the Detroit Marathon actually crosses the Detroit River into Canada, runs alongside it, then crosses back into Detroit. Even though I noticed other competitors in long sleeves, some wearing hats and gloves, I was convinced that once I got moving my body would produce more than enough heat to stay warm. After all, before moving out with a ruck on our back, even in colder weather, we drop our snivel.[42] I failed to consider the speed and the wind. At no point had I ever moved out with a ruck on my back at twenty plus miles per hour.

---

42 Military term for cold-weather clothing.

I was good out of the gate. While many participate in these events for fun, for the comradery, for the experience, I was there for one reason: to win. As we crossed the first bridge into Canada, the crosswind cut through me like a knife. I thought, "Yeah, this kinda sucks, but I'll be across in a second and good to go." I crossed, but unfortunately I had what seemed like the entire river to handrail and by the time I got to the second bridge to cross back over into Detroit, I was freezing. It was on the second bridge that I hit a decision point. Boom. Out of the blue. I could no longer feel my hands or my foot. The neoprene T-shirt I was rocking was doing precisely jack and shit to keep me warm. I began feeling my body shaking more and more uncontrollably. I was beyond pissed at myself. "Is this seriously happening?" I thought to myself as I assessed the severity of the situation. "Okay, there are safety cyclists and vehicles all over the place. I'll be fine." At this point, winning the hand cycle division was long gone. I was dropping back rapidly and quickly found myself with the "we are just going to have fun with it" crew. When I dropped behind them, I merely wanted to finish the race, and even that looked bleak.

One of the safety riders on a standard bicycle rode over to me to ask if everything was alright. "Okay, if this dude is asking me this question, I am really in rough shape," I thought. "Yeah, I am good," of course was my answer. I could have stopped. I mean, seriously, who would care? "Amputee quits Detroit Marathon due to lack of snivel" was unlikely to make the front page. But now I was pissed. Pissed at myself, but pissed nonetheless. Decision point arrived; decision made. (1) I am finishing this race if it kills me and (2) my only chance to warm up is to move faster, which will also make this misery end sooner. *Move!*

I threw everything I had into that hand crank. I blew past the "enjoy the experience" conglomerate as I accelerated along the route.

I was off the bridge, and now I had protection from the wind afforded by the buildings. I was slowly warming up. I felt good.

I did not come close to winning the division. As I crossed the finish line, I was still shaking uncontrollably. Achilles and race staff members ran over, threw a space blanket on me, and handed me my crutches. They placed a medal around my neck, we took some pictures—happiness all around, except for me. I was focused entirely on seeing straight and not toppling over. I crutched myself to the competitors' tent, where Achilles had a section blocked off for its team members. Toni was sitting there drinking a Gatorade. She had run the half-marathon event. She took one look at me and asked, "Are you alright?"

"No, I'm not," I said while laughing. I sat down. Toni grabbed me a hot chocolate and some food. "I told you to wear some warmer clothing." Perfect. Just what I wanted to hear. But she was right. And we just laughed while I attempted to avoid hypothermia.

Detroit Marathon, Detroit, MI, October 2013

WHETHER ANTICIPATED OR NOT, we must learn to leverage the crossroads—our decision points. They provide enormous opportunity to progress, and we can forecast their inevitability. They are coming. We know this with certainty. And when most people hit this point, they divert. They do what they like or what is safe, which is, of course, easy because excuses are the most convincing when facing something difficult, uncomfortable, or unpleasant. "I'll get back on track Monday." "I'll just do that instead." "I'll hit it hard tomorrow." "Just twenty more minutes and I'll get up." "I'll make up for it later." How many times have we said that, heard that, done that?

When we understand that everybody eventually hits a decision point, and that when they do most give in, our decision point becomes an opportunity. It gives us a chance to either extend our lead or make up ground on our competition. Through this understanding, we will begin to welcome these decision points. We will seek them. We will find ourselves intentionally pushing until we find ourselves standing at that crossroads, and when we arrive, when most would find themselves conflicted, we are not. We embrace it.

So when we say, "I will never leave a fallen comrade," what we are saying is, "I will do whatever it takes to make it." At times we have to ignore the brain, listen to the heart, and take the risk.

THE POWER OF LANGUAGE

The mind and the body are more intimately connected than most recognize. The body responds to what the mind says. Words have meaning, and consistent assertions, internal or verbally spoken, will have real effects within three-dimensional time and space. Simple everyday inaccurate, excuse-ridden expressions such as, "I don't have time," "It is what it is," "No matter what I do, I can't ____," or "There's always tomorrow," are killers to progress. Whether intended literally or not is irrelevant. Consciously or subconsciously, we are setting limitations on ourselves[43] and/or placing blame elsewhere (i.e., lack of ownership). When we get command of our language, we gain command of our mind: the deadliest, most capable tool within the human body.

The warrior mindset is not exclusive to those who are warriors by profession. It is a philosophy available to anybody who chooses it, and its principles as interpreted through Objective Secure are critical components within the machine of success. Train the mind and the body will follow, or as Muhammad Ali said, "If my mind can conceive it, and my heart can believe it, then I can achieve it."

---

43 As with the elephant and the rope.

SECTION 2.
STRATEGY

ARE YOU DYING TO PUT this book down and go? Perhaps you simply needed some assistance with your optics. Maybe you just lost focus there for a bit. For you, the warrior mindset was enough, and you are eager to get after it. Outstanding. Get after it. Just know there is even more here to take away.

Perhaps you are not in this camp. You are sitting there thinking, *Okay, I hear what you're saying. It makes sense and I'm on board, but I need more than that. I need something tangible—something concrete. I need a formula to follow or perhaps there is just a glitch in my current system.* I got you. That is what we are going to discuss now: the blueprint—the eight-phase process to design your reality. Let's go.

PHASE 1. MISSION

HERE IS WHERE WE IDENTIFY THE MISSION. This is the long-term goal. The dream. The "what" we are trying to accomplish, the "who" we aspire to become. There is a reason why this is Phase 1; it is exceedingly important. If we botch this, we may be making progress, but progress in the wrong direction.

———

GREEN BERETS ARE EXPECTED to be experts in land navigation—the process of moving cross-country[44] on foot while carrying anywhere from forty to one hundred pounds of gear, with nothing more than a map, protractor, and compass. This skillset is a fundamental aspect of SFAS, the SFQC, detachment training, and conducting operations. Yes, we have and utilize technology, but technology requires batteries and things break, which is why all SOF operators are

---

44   Without the use of roads or trails.

considered masters of the basics. You never know when that is all you will have available.

A critical component of SFAS is the land navigation assessment known as the STAR course—a series of five points (destinations), and therefore five legs, each anywhere from five kilometers to more than ten kilometers apart, executed in the darkness of night within a certain amount of time and starting and ending at the same point. When completed, the course resembles the shape of a star if viewed from the sky.

When it came time to conduct this exercise, physically I was ready. By this time, the required minimum weight, approximately forty-five pounds dry,[45] felt like nothing on my back. I was conditioned, my endurance capacity was high, I understood the fundamentals, and I was ready to destroy this course. The cadre issued out the grids to each of the points to the students, each with a different set and/or in a different order. We were given approximately five minutes to plot our individual routes on our maps before the time would start. Then it was on us[46] to move out. I wrote down each grid and plotted them on my map. At the five-minute mark, I was up and moving. I was not only going to finish within the allotted time, I was also going to come in first.

While moving across open terrain, I was at a light jog. While moving through thick vegetation like a draw,[47] I slowed down enough to reduce the chance of injury and/or getting off course. Boom. I hit my first point. I was well under time and off to the second point. The terrain association training we had received prior was working. I

---

45 Not including water.

46 At our discretion.

47 A terrain feature formed by two parallel ridges or spurs with low ground in between them.

could visualize where I was on my map without relying solely on my pace count.[48] Boom, point two. *Easy day. Feeling fine. Plenty of water. Legs are good to go.*

I moved to point three. I passed a few students who looked lost. Although being a team player is reinforced early, often, and aggressively throughout SFAS, some events, including the STAR course, are individual events. Any attempt to assist another student is an automatic failure and will almost certainly result in an honor code violation and a bus ride home. Good luck, brother, I said to myself and kept moving. I arrived at point three way ahead of schedule. I had just one more point to find, then I could head back to camp and call it a night. *Too easy. I am definitely in first place right now. Let's finish strong.*

I moved to point four, the shortest leg on my route. *I should be there by now. Keep moving. Maybe my legs are more tired than I thought and I am slowing down. But the vegetation wasn't that bad. I should be there by now. Recheck my point. Recheck my azimuth.*[49] *I am online. I didn't stray at all.* I had no major obstruction I had to box around. I made a classic land navigation mistake—one instructors harped on repeatedly. I began to move aimlessly. I was convinced I was at the right spot. I read the terrain and matched that to the point on the map. "It should be right here" (the last words of any land navigation student prior to failing an event). I was running around in circles, literally, feverishly searching for my point. An hour went by, then two, then three. Finally I stopped, something that was long overdue. The sun had risen over the tree line. I found some shade and took a seat. My goal to come in first was long gone. Simply finishing the

---

48 A predetermined distance according to the number of steps taken.

49 Bearing on a compass, i.e., the direction of movement.

course within the allowed time would be a stretch, and considering I was essentially lost, it was unlikely. I pulled out the piece of paper on which I had originally written the grids to my points and rechecked against the point I had plotted on the map. Like a punch to my gut, I saw my error. I had misplotted the point. I was exactly where I had intended to go. Unfortunately, my destination was approximately five hundred meters away.

I replotted my point, shot my azimuth, and took off. I knew it was going to be close, but the only option was to try. In a dead sprint. I hit point four. Just got to make it back to camp now, point 5. I was exhausted. I couldn't remember with accuracy what time we launched—the time the clock started. Did I have another seventy minutes, or another ten? Forget it. Move. I made it back to camp, the start point, point 5. Other students were moving in and out of their tents eating, performing medical treatment to their feet, and repacking their rucks. Needless to say, I did not finish first. I brought my score-card and map to the lead cadre for verification and ruck weigh-in. My points were verified, my ruck weight was above the minimum, and I was forty-five minutes over the allotted time. I had failed.

The cadre gave us five minutes to plot our points from the prescribed grids prior to starting the clock. They made clear we could move out at our leisure. It was up to us. They even reminded us to double- and triple-check our points. They could not have set us up for success any better. The problem was, I didn't listen to instruction. I was so eager to get moving, to destroy the course, to beat everybody else, that I misplotted my fourth point, a sloppy mistake that cost me.

That night, those of us who failed were given a second attempt. And while I loaded my ruck, got issued my grids, plotted them on my map, and began to move out, the students who had passed the night before were making a fire. They had the rest of the night off. I was pissed. But I had only myself to be angry with.

WHEN DETERMINING THE MISSION, we must be honest with ourselves. What do we really want? We must ask ourselves, "What do I want to do? Who do I want to be?" For some, this is a challenge within itself. Some simply feel lost.

Course of action:
1. the actions to be taken
2. a procedure adopted to deal with a situation (*Merriam-Webster*)

Course of Action (COA) 1. Reflection:
My first recommendation to determine the mission is to just sit with yourself. Daydream. Meditate. Call it what you want. Lay on the floor in a dark room, sit in a church, walk in the park. Find a location that brings solace. Recognize that oftentimes dreams do not come screaming in your face. Oftentimes they arrive in the form of a whisper. It can be quiet and difficult to hear. But if you pay attention, think, and focus, eventually you will hear it.

If this is simply not working, if you find yourself growing frustrated or antsy, if you know you want to progress but simply cannot figure out what you want to do, who you want to become, the next COA I recommend requires a shift in the question.

COA 2. Talent:
Here we seek to hone in on our talents, our gifts. Let's quickly clarify

the difference between talent and skill, as these terms are often used interchangeably, but there is a distinct difference. Talent is something we are born with. It is natural. Skill is something that comes only through hours and hours of dedication to a craft. Talent is given; skill is earned. Period.

We focus on our talents. What do we do best with the least amount of effort? This may be broad such as being athletic, outgoing, or compassionate. It also may be more specific such as cooking, repair, math, etc. What are we really good at with ease? This can provide us a direction. Chances are our talents (1) are things we enjoy and (2) provide us the best odds for success.

Once we decide on a talent, we then determine how to leverage it into a profession or lifestyle. How can I use this to better myself, my family, my community, or the world? The answer may not arrive in a single day. It may require additional thought and analysis. But it gets the ball rolling.

So why is homing in on our talents the *second* recommended course of action? That seems to make the most sense. Why not just get right to that immediately? Many speakers, coaches, and wildly successful people will recommend doing just that. Determine your talent and double down on being the best in the world at it. I agree this brings the highest chance of success, the highest chance for greatness. I am not opposed to this whatsoever. The reason why I recommend going this route as a secondary option when determining the mission is that I simply do not like the idea of restriction. I'd prefer the initial course of action be one that comes from the heart as opposed to the brain.

Admittedly, this is more than likely my competitive side coming through. I do not do well with my future being dictated to me, apparently even if that is coming from myself. "Roses are red, violets are blue, I'm a schizophrenic, and so am I." — Bob Wiley (Bill Murray), *What about Bob.*

Perhaps what or who we desire to become is something we have never considered before. Perhaps it is something we are quite terrible at in this moment. What if I have a burning desire to build homes, but can't successfully stack three blocks on top of each other without them toppling over? What if, deep down inside, my soul is screaming at me to serve my country in the military, but I can't run more than eleven feet without keeling over? Does that mean these are not options? I would argue no, it does not. The logical, calculated move is to focus on our talents. But some things in life defy logic. Some things just do not make practical sense.

We can't place too much pressure on ourselves to nail this right out of the gate. There is a likelihood that our dreams, our mission may shift. Plot your point and move out. "Perfection is the enemy of progress." — Winston Churchill.

SUMMER 2007. When I decided to enlist, my intent was simple: become a Green Beret, do my time, get out of the Army, and take those skills to the United States Secret Service (USSS). Becoming a USSS special agent was the mission, specifically on the presidential protective detail. Protective instincts and behavior are ingrained in me from both nature and nurture. The background on this is something I will get into at a later time and place, but putting myself in harm's way for another was something that came easily. I wanted to do that at the highest level. I wanted to be one of the members on the team responsible for the protection of the president of the United States.

In 2010, however, once I got to my first ODA, there was a problem. I enjoyed it. This is, of course, a strange problem to have. Following my first deployment to Afghanistan, I really caught the bug. I loved what I was doing. I had a difficult time imagining doing anything outside of the special operations community. I wanted to remain. I wanted this to become my profession rather than a means to an end. The mission now was to become the best Green Beret possible.

It was on my second deployment to Afghanistan that I again shifted the mission. This trip was direct-action focused and highly kinetic. I loved it. With every operation, I could feel my technical and tactical abilities increase. My athletic abilities through years of training and playing sports, coupled with my aggressiveness, provided me the opportunity to excel. I decided I wanted to make an attempt at joining another elite Special Operations unit.

In between operations and training, I mapped out my plan toward this new mission—the schools I would request to attend to best prepare me, the timeline, when I would request a shot at selection, how this may alter my personal life. New mission set. Objectives determined. Let's go.

This mission was short-lived. It wasn't more than a couple months later that I was in the intensive care unit at Walter Reed fighting for my life. Once again, I determined the new mission. Don't die, then get back on the team.

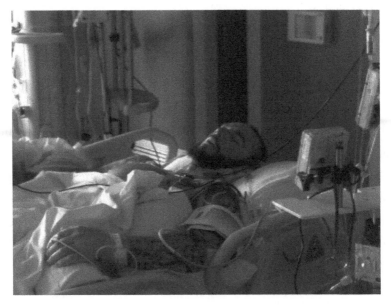

Intensive Care Unit, Walter Reed National Military
Medical Center, Bethesda, MD, March 2013

WAS THE TIME SPENT WORKING to become a USSS special agent wasted because I altered the mission? No. In fact, there was enormous value. I learned a lot. My missions changed, but they were extremely close to one another. By following my dreams, I simply fine-tuned who I wanted to become.

Once the mission has been identified, we must first recognize that progression is not linear. We are going to face challenges, many of which will beat us in the short term. We are going to get knocked on our asses. We are going to fail. We are going to have difficult moments, days, and weeks. Knowing this is inevitable, we must be prepared to overcome. One tool we can leverage is mementos.

MOVING OFTEN AS A CHILD made life challenging. I was the new kid in class just about every year. The term "bullying" has much more impact today than it did when I was growing up. Back then, it was simply part of being a kid. As a result, I was often picked on, I struggled to make and keep friends, and, believe it or not, I was tiny. So there I was—a small, scared kid. Who did I idolize? Professional athletes and the action movie stars of the 1990s.

Sylvester Stallone, Chuck Norris, Jean-Claude Van Damme, Stephen Seagal—nobody picked on these dudes. They were big and strong, they kicked ass, and they always got the girl. Another was Arnold Schwarzenegger. At that time, I didn't know much about his past. Access to information was not at our fingertips like it is today, and I was fine with just knowing he was not to be messed with and always saved the day. The Terminator, Predator, and Commando were classic entertainment for the young and motivated. It wasn't until I was in college in the early 2000s that I watched the documentary *Pumping Iron.*

My strength coach and training partner, Paul, after a brutal training session, threw it on in his apartment before whipping up a couple of protein shakes for us. At this point, I was aware that prior to becoming an action movie icon, Arnold was a bodybuilder. I had come across some of his material in magazines here and there but never gave it much thought. After seeing the documentary, I decided to look more into his evolution. What I learned is something I did not put into serious action until years later—the power of visual reminders, or as I prefer to call them, mementos.

As an adolescent and teen, Arnold would put pictures of different athletes he looked up to or emulated all over his bedroom walls. Bodybuilders, boxers, strongmen, and other athletes—he would look at them and visualize himself looking or performing the same way.

He relied on these reminders for motivation, and this technique is something he continues to stress to this day.

This, of course, is common. We see it in many places and in many forms. Pictures on walls, tattoos, jewelry—some for nostalgia, others as reminders, and yes, many for the purpose of motivation. Our museums are filled with depictions of and actual mementos dating back to the dawn of mankind. So while this is not a new concept, Arnold, an icon of mine while I was growing up, prompted my intentional use of this technique.

For me, it began pretty basically. I'd cut out pictures in fitness magazines and tape them to the walls of my bedroom. Eventually I began leveraging technology, and through my research discovered various quotes that inspired me. Screen shot, print, and display. Eventually, my mementos spread throughout my home. Then into my truck. Then into my locker and desk at work. When I felt things getting really tough, I would tape one of these to my cell phone before going to sleep. That way, when my alarm went off at some ungodly hour, I had to physically get past that reminder in order to hit the snooze button. I incorporated whiteboards, one of my all-time favorite inventions. Through the use of these, even if I am writing a word, or phrase, or famous quote from somebody else, because I am writing it, with that comes ownership and a quick but firm contract I establish with myself.

I utilize these practices to this day. Fortunately, my wife gets it and is okay with the picture of Jocko Willink taped to the inside of a cabinet door in the kitchen. These reminders are essential components. I depend on them. Yes, there will be plenty of days when we spring up, happy, excited, good to go without the need for any external assistance whatsoever. There will also be many, possibly more often than not, when we are worn down but know we must put in the work regardless.

———————

THE CONTRACT WE ESTABLISHED during the introduction of this journey doubles as a memento. Leverage it. The key to leveraging mementos is preparation. These reminders absolutely must be in place *before* you need them. Because after ten hours of sleep, or while on vacation, or when everything is great at work or at home, you don't need them. When you set your mind toward a new mission or objective, you're excited and you wake up hungry. On the first day at the new job, day one of a new nutrition plan, the first day at school, things are good. You feel good. Motivation is high. You're excited. Again, you don't need them. But how about when you are tired, beat up, sore, or going through a rough patch with your spouse, or child, or boss? How about when you have been grinding for a week, or a month, or a year? How about when the monotony sets in and the thing you used to be excited about doing is now something you can no longer stand? *This* is when your mementos serve their purpose. This is when that photograph of the dream home or the motivational quote pays dividends—when things are hard.

Identifying the mission requires brutal honesty with ourselves. Remember, this is what or who *we* want to become.

PHASE 2. DESIGN

WE MUST HAVE A SOLID UNDERSTANDING of our current situation, our mission, our obstacles, and how we are going to advance. This may sound intimidating. Do not let this overwhelm you. It is actually quite simple.

STEP 1: Determine our current situation. Where are we right now? Not physically, but conceptually. "I am in my kitchen," is irrelevant. This may begin as simple as, "I am unhappy with my current profession," or "The home I live in is unsatisfactory." From there, I challenge you to take it a level deeper. We must ask ourselves why. What is it I dislike about my job? What exactly is the problem with where I live? Think about it. Then annotate it.[50]

---

50 For presentation purposes, we will use "New Home" as the example mission for our Design model.

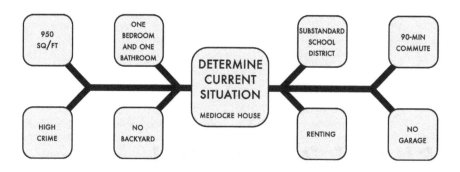

STEP 2: Define the mission. This is the mission we have already determined. If we were having difficulty determining this, here is another opportunity for refinement. Our deep thought into our current situation will help us hone in on this. Annotate it.

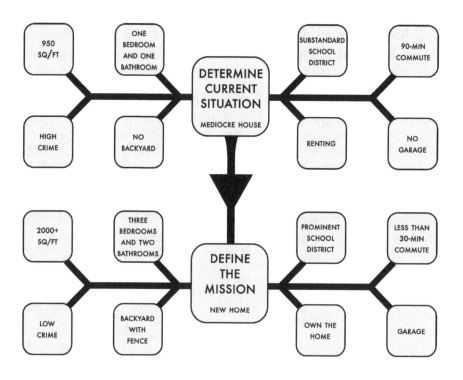

STEP 3: Frame the problem. Here we determine the obstacles impeding our progress toward the desired end state. The "I am not ___," "I need ___," etc. What is standing in between us and mission success? Annotate them.

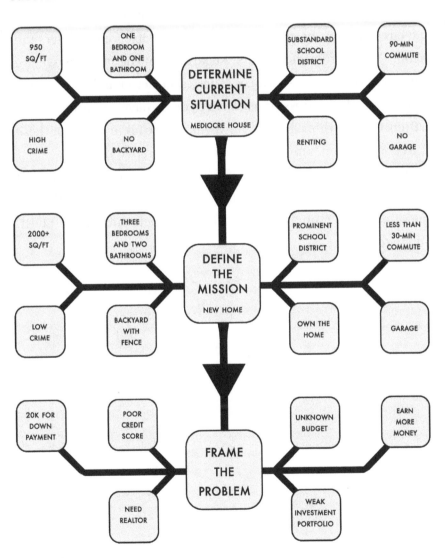

STEP 4: Identify our lines of effort (LOEs). Here we determine what broad, general categories require action to resolve the problem(s). Think conceptually, for example: athletic ability, intelligence, education, financial, social, etc. The keys are (1) keep them broad, (2) be honest with ourselves, and (3) consider everything. It is easy to focus solely on the specifics of the mission itself and neglect the second- and third-order effects. Regardless of the mission, we are going to have to make sacrifices. These sacrifices will have a ripple effect. Time, sleep, stress—the list can go on for days. We are *not* going to think of everything. Ideally, however, we are taking some of these into consideration here in order to be better prepared.

These categories are our LOEs. To all my military scholars out there: yes, there is a difference between lines of effort and lines of operation. For simplicity's sake, we are going to simply use LOEs. Annotate them.

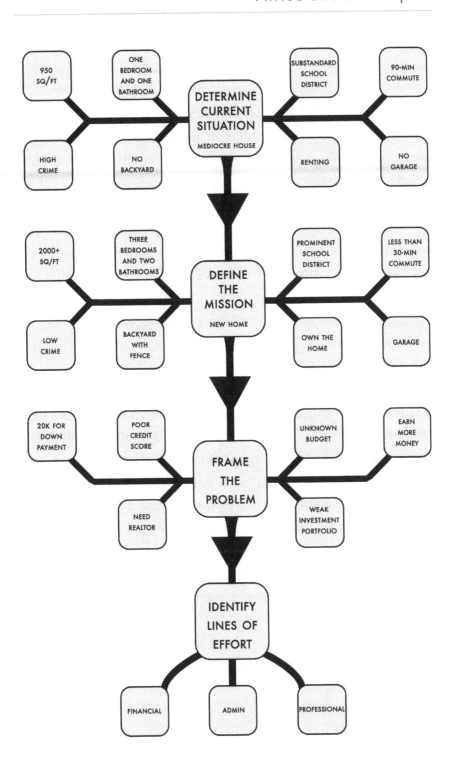

WHILE YOU ARE ON INPATIENT STATUS, your hospital room seems to have a revolving door on it. Different medical specialists and department staff members are constantly circulating through to do their checks and to implement interventions as needed. One of these specialists is a psychologist.

Typically, a couple of times a week, one of the psychs would come into my room to check up on my status. Psychs ask a variety of questions. It is relatively straightforward. Even in my ketamine- and post-anesthesia-induced condition, again, I knew what my intentions were: getting back to the team. I can remember clearly voicing this to the psychs several times. I honestly didn't see anything unusual about it.

April 2013. My father tells this story better than I do, as I heard it only secondhand, but on one particular day, a psych came in to visit me, and I had just been wheeled out for surgery. My father told the doc the deal, and they began talking a bit. The psych explained to my father that I was continuously talking about returning to my job on an SF detachment, doing the same things I had done before, etc. He further explained to my father that he felt I was perhaps in a state of shock or denial or, simply due to the drugs, not yet aware of the severity of my situation. He essentially warned my father that at some point I would be made aware of how badly I was injured and that the likelihood of me doing what I intended to do was extraordinarily unlikely, perhaps impossible. He simply wanted my father to be prepared to deal with what could potentially be a dramatic and severe fall into depression.

In hindsight, I may have had the same thoughts and concerns as he did. After all, I was on an enormous amount of medication, I was in surgery three times a week, and my expressed intentions were unprecedented. Additionally, I am positive he had seen this cause and effect happen throughout his medical career. So I get it. No hard feelings, doc.

My father expressed his appreciation for the information and analysis before telling the psych that he didn't see that as likely to happen. My father explained that he felt I knew what was going on, I had amazingly accepted the reality of my situation, and just as quickly had already focused on the next evolution. He told the doc, "This is just who Nick is."

My father knows me as well as anybody. He is my best friend in this world. He knew that I knew my current situation and that even while doped up with enough pain killers and anesthesia to kill a horse, I was already formulating a plan.

THE PIECES ARE COMING TOGETHER. The puzzle is not assembled, but we are close.[51]

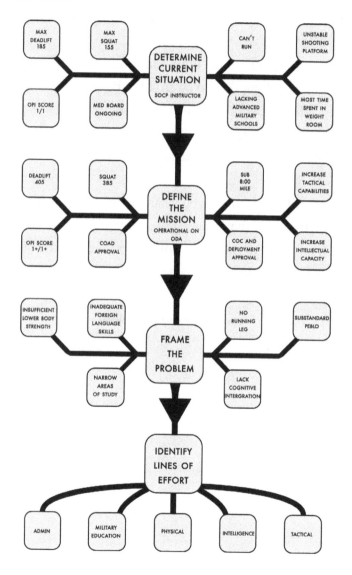

---

51   This is a depiction of the Design model I developed upon my return to Fort Bragg once discharged from Walter Reed hospital. The mission: Return to Operational Status.

PHASE 3. RESEARCH

ACCESS TO INFORMATION has never been as readily available as it is today—never! There is absolutely no excuse to be uninformed. "I dunno how," is just that: an excuse, an avoidable reason. We must set ourselves up for success. The key to this phase, however, is to move quickly. We cannot get stuck here. The research is solely to get the wheels spinning and provide some direction to advance down our lines of effort.

———

HIGH OUTPUT WITH LOW RETURN on investment (ROI) is frustrating. I have lost track of how many times I felt as though I was giving it one hundred percent but was just not seeing the results. When this happens to us, we have the control to make adjustments as needed, to work the trial-and-error process. When we are witness to this happening to someone else, however, we do not. We can advise if/ when appropriate, but, depending on the individual, the timing, the delivery, and a host of additional variables, our advice may fall on deaf ears. As an individual who believes deeply in the work, in the effort, I find this scenario among the most frustrating to experience.

Since my time in SF, we have had our own training facilities. The equipment is state of the art, and the sole purpose of the world-class staff is to increase our physical abilities. And while I, to this day, spend a substantial amount of time here, I have always also conducted some of my training at other locations. There are a few reasons for this; however, at the top is simply a desire for a change of venue. In SF, we spend a considerable amount of time with each other. This is, of course, essential for the development of cohesive teams; however, time away, and in my case during physical training, time alone, is also important.

One of these training facilities on Fort Bragg is called the Ritz-Epps Physical Fitness Center. It was and, as far as I am aware, it is still what we would refer to as a "meathead gym." Dumbbells, barbells, a sea of machines used to isolate specific muscle groups, and mirrors on just about every wall. It was home to many athletes who competed on stage and to patrons with exquisitely coordinated workout attire and accessories.

Since the anticipated introduction of the new Army Combat Fitness Test (ACFT), most physical fitness centers on army installations center around "functional fitness."[52] Ritz-Epps is a place to go when you want to clang and bang / get swole / bro lift / sling lead / jack steel / get a pump / look good naked.

Sometime in mid-2016, I went into Ritz-Epps one afternoon after work. About halfway through my training session, a young man

---

52 A commonly misused term, and something to discuss in another forum.

approached me in between sets.[53] Let's call him Brian. Brian was extremely respectful and simply wanted to thank me for providing him with some motivation. As always, I was appreciative. We exchanged some small talk, he asked if we could take a selfie together, which I obliged, and he left.

Over the course of the following months I would notice Brian in the gym. He couldn't have been older than twenty. He was a skinny, unassuming specialist (E4 rank) in the 82nd Airborne, and from what I noticed he always trained alone. I also noticed Brian trained hard. He was clearly a novice weightlifter and his form needed development, but this kid went all out. We'd exchange the standard gym nod or fist bump and kept it at that. He and I were both in there to work.

Later that year, my detachment and I deployed to Somalia. Upon our return in early 2017, I eventually made my way back into Ritz-Epps to train. My first day back there, who do I see? Brian. It was very easy to spot him. Not only was he training in a Brian-like manner, a.k.a. going balls to the wall with at best moderate control, but he hadn't changed a bit. By this point, at least eight months had passed since I last saw him. And when I say no change, I mean literally no change whatsoever. I could feel my frustration building.

For the duration of my workout, I struggled with the idea of approaching him to talk. I was confident he would at least hear me out, but I feared I would embarrass him. I decided to hold off until the appropriate time presented itself.

---

53 If you are going to initiate a conversation with somebody in the gym, ensure it is in between sets. I have lost track of how many times somebody has started talking to me while I was literally moving weights. Gym etiquette, people. It's a thing.

I lost track of him during my training session, but I made a mental note to address this whenever possible. As I was making my way to my truck following my workout, I heard somebody call out to me. I looked into the driver's seat of the car parked next to me, and, sure enough, it was Brian. We exchanged greetings. He asked where I had been and was somewhat blown away when I said, "Somalia," before I asked him if he had a few minutes to talk. He answered in the affirmative and I walked around and sat in his passenger seat.

Brian was more than a little confused. In fact, I'd say he was outright scared, even if only for a second. I broke the ice by telling him if I wanted to hurt him it wouldn't be in such a crowded parking lot. I asked him what his goals were for training. "Why are you coming to the gym?" He stated, embarrassed, that he wanted to get bigger; he wanted to put on muscle. I wasn't exactly surprised by his answer. I then asked him what his program looked like. He looked at me like I had just asked him the square root of something. "What is your split? What is your macro rotation? It is periodized? What set/rep scheme are you using?" Brian now looked at me as if I were speaking Persian/Farsi. I laughed and told him not to feel bad; we just had a little work to do.

Brian and I spent the next thirty minutes talking about physical training programming, a few rock-solid principles and techniques that have been solidified over the years but, more importantly, the importance of programming itself. I explained I could see he clearly had the heart, and that is something that is extremely difficult to teach. Some would argue it is impossible to teach. The drive was there. The work ethic was there. He just needed some organization and understanding of why he was doing what he was doing. "A man cannot understand the art he is studying if he only looks for the end result without taking the time to delve deeply into the reasoning of the study." —Miyamoto Musashi

I took Brian's email address and, over the following few weeks, put together a training program and nutrition plan for him to follow. He was grateful. He offered to pay me, which I, of course, declined immediately. I told him, "Your progress is the only payment I am interested in, and now you owe me."

In July 2017, I transferred from 3rd SFG(A) on Fort Bragg to 5th SFG(A) on Fort Campbell. Yes, this is rare. The short version of the story is Toni, also active-duty Army, came down on orders for 5th SFG(A); therefore I transferred groups. It wasn't until October 2018 that I would return to Fort Bragg to attend some training. As per standard operating procedure (SOP), I began training at Ritz-Epps two or three times per week. Around my third or fourth time there, I walked in and boom. Brian was knocking out a set of standing dumbbell military presses, a unique exercise but a standard in all of my programming. Brian had put on at least twenty pounds within the eighteen months since I had last seen him. He had ditched the oversized white T-shirt and basketball shorts and found himself a pair of Ranger panties and a cutoff. Clothing aside, he looked great. Additional muscle mass aside, he looked confident, and this had me beaming like a proud father.

I settled onto a bench near the dumbbell rack. I had a fight with some incline presses in my immediate future, but I had difficulty focusing. Fortunately, this time Brian spared me the decision-making process by walking over to me immediately. After the standard introductory small talk, I told him that he looked awesome. Brian went on a frantic tangent about the program, some things he added, some things he felt were not working, his current PRs (personal records)—the dude was glowing. I was genuinely happy for him and made that clear to him directly. Brian then got real serious, his smile disappeared, and he extended his hand. As I shook it, he looked me dead in the eyes and simply said, "Thank you, Sir." I assured Brian that the pleasure was mine and he had paid his debt.

I have returned to Fort Bragg several times for conferences and/or training since that day. However, I have not seen Brian since. There are a variety of possible reasons for this, but regardless, "Brian," if you are reading this, I wish you well, brother, and thank you for allowing me to be a small part of your journey."

SO WE HAVE OUR LINES OF EFFORT (LOEs). That is the focus behind our research. If we identified that one of our LOEs is education, and for you that means obtaining a bachelor's degree, the research provides information on how to do that. What schools are options? What resources do you need? How much will it cost? This will bleed over, and therefore, you will need to adjust your financial LOE, assuming that was already identified. If it wasn't, perhaps now it is. How many hours per week will you need to dedicate to your studies? This will bleed over, and therefore, you will need to adjust your social or family LOE. More to follow on this in a second.

During our research, the goal is to simply identify the things or tasks we have to accomplish and/or consider. Just list them. Do not worry about where and when they will require attention. Do not worry about the timeline. We are simply collecting data.

Information is important. We need some sort of guide to get things going in the right direction. But we cannot fall victim to the paralysis by overanalysis syndrome.

I will warn you now—this phase can easily become the number one excuse. "I just don't know enough yet." If we wait for the perfect time to do anything, we will be waiting indefinitely. There is no perfect time, and we will never know it all. Do not become stagnant here. *Get. To. Work.*

PHASE 4. APPROACH

THIS IS WHERE WE CREATE OUR APPROACH. We have already determined our long-term goal, our mission, our three-hundred-meter target. We have also identified our lines of effort (LOEs), the broad, conceptual categories along which we will advance. In Phase 4, we are going to implement the list of tasks/considerations we identified through our research, the series of short-term goals that exist between where we are and where we are trying to go along our LOEs. These are our objectives, our twenty-five-, fifty-, one hundred-, and two hundred-meter targets. Here is where we prioritize, organize, and correlate them along a time line.

PRIORITIZE

Prioritize:
1. to list or rate in order of priority (*Merriam-Webster*)

First let's prioritize these objectives. The highest-prioritized objectives we will refer to as decisive points (DP). Doctrinally, a DP is a geographic place, specific event, critical factor, or function that, when acted upon, allows commanders to gain a marked advantage over an adversary or to contribute materially to achieving success. Everybody and everything in your way is the adversary. Simply circle or highlight what we have identified as DPs.

ORGANIZE

Organize:

1. to form into a coherent unity or functioning whole
2. to set up an administrative structure for
3. to arrange by systematic planning and united effort
   (*Merriam-Webster*)

Next, let's organize our objectives and DPs. One LOE at a time, we determine what needs to happen in what order. For example, along our education LOE, we must find a school before we can apply; perhaps we must take some sort of entrance exam before we can enroll; maybe we need to gather some resources before we can start class. Step by step. Sequential objectives. These can be as large or small as you choose. Just know that with larger objectives there will be more tasks associated with reaching Objective Secure. Every single task does not necessarily have to be mapped out. Annotating "brush teeth" is likely a waste of time. It is implied. Find a decent balance and, again, be prepared to adjust/add/remove detail as necessary.

TIMELINE

Timeline:

1. a schedule of events and procedures (*Websters'*)

Next, let's lay out our objectives and DPs along a timeline. Now when it comes to our timeline, we *do not* have to determine days, weeks, months, or years along our lines of effort (LOEs) *immediately*. However, it is not bad practice to determine a rough estimate. There is something to be said about marking a future day on the calendar and deciding, "This is the day." It holds us accountable. It is beneficial. We do want to get to this point, and perhaps we are there now, but some missions will take years to accomplish. Most, in fact, will take longer than we would prefer. However, it simply may take some time working through the process to determine with any sort of accuracy what that timeline looks like. By all means, set days and weeks along your LOEs now. Just be prepared to expand your timeline and/or adjust as necessary. This will *not* become our excuse to procrastinate. "Oh, well, according to my approach, I was going to get this done by the end of the month, but I really just don't feel like doing that right now, so I will just extend my timeline by another month." Negative. All stop. Proceed directly to Section 1. Mindset, and get yourself straight.

CORRELATE

Correlate:

1. either of two things so related that one directly implies or is complementary to the other
2. a phenomenon that accompanies another phenomenon,

is usually parallel to it, and is related in some way to it
(*Merriam-Webster*)

Once we have each LOE mapped out with our objectives and deci-sive points (DP), let's correlate them to each other. As we discussed, if we determine the cost to enroll in school is X dollars, and this is something we cannot afford at the moment, we must not only priori-tize obtaining the funds necessary, we also must place this DP, along our financial LOE, *before* the "enroll" objective. Now we know that, although we may be able to advance along the education and finan-cial LOEs concurrently, we will hit a point when we can no longer advance along the education LOE without reaching Objective Secure at the "Save X dollars for school" DP.

Our correlation between LOEs, objectives, and DPs helps us main-tain our focus in the right direction. It helps us prioritize our time and effort. There is *always* something that can be done, but again, we want a solid ROI.

In Phase 4, we are identifying what needs to happen sequentially, or at least what we think needs to happen sequentially. We are using our research to determine our objectives and how we progress to Objective Secure.

We have a simple, easy-to-digest, conceptual model of where we are, where we are going, and how we are going to get there. Retain this product. This is something we will continuously revisit. While a cocktail napkin in crayon will work, I recommend taking the time to create a digital product that is simple to adjust. This is a living document—an organism. It doesn't have to be fancy. This is for you. But be prepared to modify this over time. I also recommend printing it out and having it readily available to reference daily. This alone is a powerful memento, assuming it doesn't overwhelm us. This is simply a tool, a spreadsheet. If you are solely focused on one LOE at the moment, try referencing that only daily. We will discuss focus here shortly. The point is, we need to have our approach outlined for us in a clear, concise, and available manner to minimize distraction and wasted movement. We need some structure.

> *As I lay in my hospital bed at Walter Reed, knowing the goal, I quickly realized that no matter how hard I worked, how many hours I spent in the gym, I was not going to have the same physical abilities I once had. If I was seriously going to make a play at getting back onto my team, I knew I had to make up ground. I had to increase my value in other areas.*

As we find ourselves within the Fourth Industrial Revolution—the ongoing automation of traditional manufacturing and industrial practices via technology—we also find ourselves being forced to adjust, modify, or reinvent ourselves altogether. As I sit here today, in the fall of 2020, the year of COVID-19, industries have been forced to find new and innovative ways to remain relevant, stay in business, and/or continue to provide services. Many of these practices are here to stay. Although forced, companies have seen the value brought through these pivots. Perhaps COVID was simply the catalyst for the inevitable, the primer that only accelerated our "Industry 4.0."

For many, this change is unsettling. This is, of course, understandable and expected, considering that change tends to be unsettling, even when we pursue it intentionally. We fear it, run from it, fight it. We like what we know, and new is hard. But the reality is, if we are to remain relevant and remain in the game, we must adapt.

"According to Darwin's Origin of Species, it is not the most intellectual of the species that survives; it is not the strongest that survives;

but the species that survives is the one that is able best to adapt and adjust to the changing environment in which it finds itself."—Leon C Megginson, Professor of Management and Marketing, Louisiana State University, 1963. In other words, adapt or die.

———

MY PLAN TO GET BACK INTO THE ODA BEGAN UGLY. I knew there were a lot of things I needed to do, but I hadn't a clue as to how I was going to do them or if I would even be allowed to try, so I just started doing stuff. There is a lot to be learned through trial and error, but I know with certainty I would have been more efficient with some structure. I know this because once I attended the Special Warfare Operational Design Course (ODC) in 2014, learned these techniques, and applied them, my progress skyrocketed.

ODC is a course designed to teach mission and campaign planning up to the strategic level. The intended audience is the more senior members of the SOF community. As a staff sergeant, I needed a waiver to attend, but I was certain this skill set would help me increase my value to the detachment. For five weeks, alongside a bunch of sergeants major, chief warrant officers 3, majors, and lieutenant colonels, I learned the principles of operational art and design. I was smack in the middle of this course when a lightbulb went off in my head. I could use these practices to reach my real-world end state. While, as a class, we applied these methodologies to both real-world and fabricated military problem sets, I was concurrently applying them to myself, to getting back onto the detachment.

Upon completion of the course, my design was looking solid. It was clean, easy to follow, with what I felt was just the right amount of detail. Now it was time to apply it. My lines of effort (LOE)s were :

Military Education: Here is where I racked and stacked (prioritized) the various military schools and training I would seek to attend—ones that would expand my capital through the introduction of new capabilities.

Physical: Here are the major physical assessments I needed to complete in order to be cleared to return to the team. Preparation for these is something we will get into in a bit. The bottom line is that ambitious would be an understatement.

Intelligence: Here is where I placed my civilian schooling[54] and other areas of study within subjects like culture, foreign policy, clan and tribal dynamics, etc., and my foreign language skills.

Administrative: This was full of a lot of unknowns as I initially did not know what the process would be to remain on active duty and eventually back to the team, but I was certain there would be objectives and DPs. This is something I populated over time throughout the process, which subsequently forced me to modify my entire approach and timeline.

Tactical:[55] Here I focused on my shoot, move, and communicate— tasks I knew would need a lot of work. As it would turn out, I did not consider a variety of tasks. More to follow.

I had been doing a lot of these things already. But once I incorporated the operational design model, everything became clearer. Everything was integrated. It was systematic. It made sense. It helped with my focus, it helped reduce stress, and it increased my motivation, because suddenly my goal did not seem quite so impossible. I could do this. One Objective Secure at a time.

---

54 I began pursuing my master's degree in psychology.

55 Combat specific training.

LINES OF EFFORT

TIME
2014 - 2015

	AUG	SEP	OCT	NOV	DEC	JAN	FEB	MAR	APR	MAY	JUN	JUL

MILITARY EDUCATION
SLC — ODC — SOCP

PHYSICAL
APFT — 12-MILE RUCK — UBRR — SOCOM — ORT

INTELLIGENCE
GRAD SCHOOL — DPI
SEMESTER 1 — COGNITIVE ASSESSMENT
INFLUENCE, THE PSYCHOLOGY OF PERSUASION — TIPPING POINT — BLINK
SEMESTER 2 — COGNITIVE ASSESSMENT
AFGHANISTAN: A CULTURAL AND POLITICAL HISTORY
COGNITIVE ASSESSMENT — DPI
HOW TO WIN FRIENDS AND INFLUENCE PEOPLE — THE FOREVER WAR

ADMINISTRATIVE
MEB — COAD — MEDICAL — COC APPROVAL — DEPLOYMENT WAIVER

TACTICAL
AIRBORNE RECERTIFICATION — SFAUC — PATROL BASE — DRIVERS RECERTIFICATION

GLOSSARY

Military Education

SLC – Senior Leaders Course

ODC – Special Warfare Operational Design Couse

SOCP – Special Operations Combatives Program Instructor Course

Physical

APFT – Army Physical Fitness Test

UBRR – Upper Body Round Robin

SOCOM – Special Operations Command Physical Assessment

ORT – Operator Readiness Test

Intelligence

OPI – Oral Proficiency Interview, a verbal test to determine foreign language capability

Titles of different books I decided to read and study

Administrative

MEB – Medical Evaluation Board

COAD – Continuation on Active Duty

COC – Chain of Command

Tactical

Airborne Recertification – Display my ability to continue conducting airborne operations

SFAUC – Special Forces Advanced Urban Combat

Patrol Base – Living and operating within austere rural, vegetated environments

Drivers Recertification – Display my ability to operate military and non-standard vehicles

To round out the "New House" example Design model, here is a "New House" Approach model:

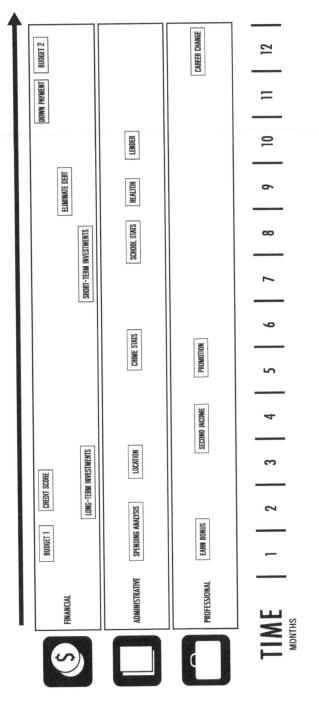

PHASE 5. EXECUTE

THERE IS A REASON WHY this is Phase 5 of 8—at the center—because it is the nucleus of the strategy.

DISCIPLINE

Discipline:
1. control gained by enforcing obedience or order
2. training that corrects, molds, or perfects the mental faculties or moral character (*Merriam-Webster*)

Discipline is controlled behavior. In other words, it is the combination of sacrifice and time prioritization. (Warrior Ethos 1: I will always place the mission first.) With discipline, we are stopping ourselves from doing things we *like/want* to do *and/or* forcing ourselves to do things we *need* to do.

There is a relationship between what we *like* to do, *want* to do, and *need* to do. If we only do what we *want* to do, we will not make the kind of progress necessary to achieve the goal. Sleeping in until eleven, eating pizza every night, or playing video games all day while crushing beers is almost certainly not going to get it done.

At the same time, if we do only what we *need* to do, life will more than likely be miserable. It will be a chore. It doesn't matter who you are, the most disciplined person on earth spends at least some time doing things he/she *likes and wants* to do.

Therefore, we must incorporate both what we *want* and *need* to do into the system.

Here is the progression:

First off, when we limit our wants, we increase their value. It may be tough to stop ourselves from playing video games every day and use that time to do something we *need* to do, but when we then allow ourselves to play that game on, say, Sunday night, we will enjoy it much more. The value of that activity has increased, and we can have guilt-free enjoyment knowing it was earned.

Eventually—and this is when things seriously take off—our needs become wants regardless of what we like. Warning: this is reserved for those with the highest degree of focus.

We may still dislike the act, but the desire for what the act creates will supersede the dislike for the act itself. Therefore, we want to do it. We may not like it, but we want to do it anyway.

For example, we want to eat pizza because we like it. If we like pizza, we will probably always like pizza, but after staying disciplined and seeing the effects of eating healthy foods instead, we want the effect more than we want the pizza.

What we see in the mirror, the compliments we get from friends or family, the confidence we now have, not feeling like crap, whatever it is— *that* will become what we need, the effect. Therefore, although we may always *like* pizza, we no longer *want* pizza, because we *need* the results.

We don't want to read because we don't like doing it. If we dislike reading, we may always dislike reading, but after staying disciplined, forcing ourselves to do it, and seeing the effects of that increase in knowledge, the increase in awareness, the ability to not only remain in complex conversations but also contribute, the effect will become what we need. Therefore, although we may *dislike* reading, we will *want* to read, because we *need* the results.

To be a successful athlete, you must push yourself to and through pain. Few people actually like pain, but successful athletes recognize the significance of that pain; therefore they want it, because, again, they *need* the results.

We may not like it, we may never like it, but eventually we will or will not want to do it anyway because we need the results.

PRIOR TO LOSING MY LEG, I was somewhere in the neighborhood of seventy percent brawn and thirty percent brain. My physical capabilities were what I brought to the table. I was big, strong, fast, and had a solid hand-to-hand fighting background. I took quickly to the tactics and techniques of CQB. It made sense to me. I enjoyed it. My team needed what I was good at, what I liked to do. It was a win-win. Lying in the hospital, I realized I would have to make an adjustment.

The constant traffic in and out of your hospital room can be quite frustrating, to be honest. In addition to that, you also typically have family members, colleagues, and friends coming and going. Some are there for the longer term, some just for a few hours. As surprising as it may seem, even that can be frustrating. And in addition to that, you also typically have DVs who come to pay their respects. This ranges from professional athletes to politicians, celebrities, etc. While I had many DVs come see me during my time in the hospital, Lieutenant General (LTG) Charles Cleveland was the most impactful.

Some DVs are experienced when it comes to visiting wounded service members. They have it down to a science. They are comfortable within the setting. Most, however, are nervous. They are unsure what to say and what topics to discuss, and most prioritize expressing gratitude and/or empathy for what the wounded individual is experiencing. There is, of course, nothing wrong with this whatsoever. I can relate. It has taken me several reps of bedside visits to become even half decent at it. And I, unlike most, have the advantage of knowing what things are like as the patient. My guess is LTG Cleveland had done this several times before coming to see me. He was, after all, the USASOC commander at the time and, therefore, had been in leadership positions since the global war on terror began, including serving as the Tenth Special Forces Group Commander from 2001 to 2003, when he led the initial invasion into northern Iraq during Operation Iraqi Freedom. Odds are he, unfortunately, had done this before.

Oftentimes, prior to a DV visit, the advanced echelon (ADVON) arrives to essentially prep the environment for the DV. When LTG Cleveland entered my room, it was unannounced. The dude just strolled in, introduced himself to my father, introduced himself to me, and pulled up a chair. It caught me completely off guard. After we exchanged some small talk, he politely asked my father to leave the room so he and I could talk privately. This was a first for me. Not only did a three-star general just casually and randomly stroll into my room, but he asked my father to kick rocks. He had my interest, to say the least.

The general pulled a small publication from his briefcase. It wasn't more than twenty pages. It looked and felt like a magazine. It was an early draft of ARSOF 2022.

ARSOF (Army Special Operations Forces) 2022 is a blueprint for change. It describes the precepts and imperatives that will enable the ARSOF to thrive in a future operating environment characterized by uncertainty. This document served as an azimuth for decision makers to advance the ARSOF.

After explaining the concept, the general asked what I thought about it. I do not recall my response; however, I am sure when factoring in my pain management medications as well as my inexperience within SOF, it was less than impressive. More important, though, was my limited understanding of the model of the direction the ARSOF was going. I do not think this was the general's intent, but it provided me options: options to remain relevant, options to remain an asset, avenues that I could pursue in order to increase my value.

As ARSOF 2022 touches on, the SF have a wide range of core tasks. In other words, we have several types of missions we are expected to execute. Direct Action (DA), the term used in the context of military special operations for small-scale raids, ambushes, sabotage, or similar actions, is more than likely what most Green Berets are drawn to. It is why we went to SFAS in the first place. It is what we prefer to do—me included. We must also be proficient in a variety of other mission sets, all of which maintain a balance between the physical and human domains. It is within this balance that I saw opportunity.

Much of what special forces do revolves around relationship development—influence. Winning the hearts and minds of an indigenous force, key leaders, other government agencies, and/or the local populace. It was here that I would make my move. I was confident that increasing my capability within this sphere would increase my value and make up some of the physical abilities ground I had lost.

I started immediately after the general left my room, beginning with reading the not yet public ARSOF 2022 he had left for me to reference. From there, I expanded my reading and research into the works of people like Robert Cialdini, Malcolm Gladwell, and many others who focus on the social and psychological spheres. For the remainder of my time at Walter Reed, my studies were a top priority.

Upon my arrival back to Bragg, and once settled into my role as a combatives instructor, I pursued specific schools and training that focused on these skills. I stuck out like a sore thumb (e.g., as in the Special Warfare Operational Design Course). I began working toward my master's degree in psychology. I continued the expansion of my reading into these fields. And at no point did I like any of it. Like much of my work with Kelly, it was boring. I would have rather been reading about strength training or nutrition. I would have rather been at the range working on my marksmanship or tactical reloads. I would have rather been on the mats drilling my half guard to side control transitions. But I was certain it would pay off. It was what I needed to do. Turns out, I was right.

IT IS HARD. It's supposed to be hard. It is work. It is supposed to be work. But like Jocko says, "discipline equals freedom," or, more exactly, it is the path that leads to freedom because through discipline we are able to do whatever we want, become whatever we want. Everybody has moments of weakness when the excuses and justifications start coming in, and in these moments, remember that everybody comes to the crossroad and when they do, most people give in. So if everybody gets to this point, and most people cave, these crossroads become our opportunities to advance. Remember that. This is critical. This is our moment. All the work we have put in up to this point hinges on this decision. And when we do the right thing, and stay on track despite the temptation, we will start looking forward to these moments, these tests of willpower. We will feed off of them and start talking to ourselves, even yelling at a slice of pizza. "Oh, you think you can beat *me*?!? Nope, not today, not this time!!" We cannot win the war against the world if we cannot win the battle within our own mind. When we remain disciplined, we relinquish immediate satisfaction for long-term self-respect.

THE WORDS OF TREY PACE

Upon returning home from an eight-month deployment to Afghanistan, I was interviewing for a job at the 3rd Special Forces Group combatives committee as a full-time combatives instructor. When I walked into the office to meet with the noncommissioned officer in charge (NCOIC), I was a little intimidated. Sitting behind the desk was one of the largest human beings I had ever seen. Covered in tattoos and sweat from a prior workout, Nick Lavery looked up at me from his protein shake. "What's up, bro?" he said in his booming Boston accent. I explained that I was looking for the NCOIC and that I wanted to try to get a position working on the combatives committee.

"Too easy. Give me a minute." He stood up, hopped past me to the door, and yelled down the hallway with a voice that seemed to shake the rafters, "Yo, Josh, Trey's heaahh!" I couldn't help but notice he had only one leg. As I talked to Josh, I overheard Nick explaining to one of our coworkers, as he was strapping on his prosthetic leg, how the workout he had just completed had crushed him but it was time to go teach warriors how to fight. I remember thinking to myself, *Holy shit! This guy just finished a workout, and now he's going to fight with Green Berets on the mats for the rest of the day.* I knew right then that if I was going to work here, I had to step up my game to another level.

When you are working next to Nick Lavery, finding motivation to level up becomes pretty easy. Fast-forward to about a month later after I was hired as the primary Modern Army Combatives Program (MACP) instructor—my dream job. I got into the office at about 0700, thinking I would make a good impression by showing up early. To my surprise, someone was already there. I opened the door and Nick was leaning back on the couch, covered in sweat, trying to catch his breath. "Good morning, brother."

So much for my good impression. Long story short, this guy had gotten to the gym at around 0530, had worked out for an hour and a half, and was now pulling out what looked like a half-gallon home-made shake and a bucket of egg whites from his giant lunch bag with about five other large Tupperware containers waiting to be micro-waved. Most people would think, *Yeah, he got his workout in early and ate some food after so he doesn't have to do it later; that's pretty normal.* What they don't realize is that this was the first of three to four workouts that day, not to mention the thirty-minute calisthenics and yoga session that he would do at home right after he woke up.

Another thing I would like to point out about Nick is that he would program the whole team's nutrition and strength/conditioning programs individually and make sure we were executing the plans he laid out for us, all while getting in his own specific programming tailored to return him to an ODA. The year I worked with Nick on the committee, I can honestly say, completely changed the way I thought about life, not only in my own training as a BJJ athlete but also in the way I approach problems and people outside of training. Nick has a way of instilling certain values and a work ethic into people around him without having to say a word. It's not just because he is missing a leg and still works like a machine. It's his mindset. Discipline for Nick seems to come naturally. It seems like he doesn't even have to try to be motivated to go about the day. He just is. He just does it.

For a long time while working with him, I didn't even know he was trying to return to operational status. It's not something he talked about a lot, which, to me, really highlights his humility. Nick didn't really talk about his own personal goals. For the most part, he wanted to talk only about *your* goals and what *you* were doing to achieve them. You could always tell there was a fire burning, though. He was in training for something. The man attacked training like a crazy person—all business. If it wasn't one of his return-to-duty assessments, it was a local grappling tournament. If not that, it was an MMA fight or the All Armed Forces Combatives Tournament. He focused on his professional development as a combatives instructor by completing the SOCP instructor course, the first amputee to do so ever. Nick maintained an unbelievable balance between remaining selfless in order to propel the people around him, while also demanding his own development, a skill I still try to emulate today in my life.

One of the most memorable and rewarding experiences I have had in Brazilian Jiu Jitsu (BJJ) is when Nick and I would work through certain positions and techniques we modified to Nick's abilities on the mats. We were constantly trying to make little adjustments and nuances to traditional fighting techniques, and I was extremely impressed by his ability to not only learn the new techniques but also to execute them in live sparring with zero hesitation. Undoubtedly, the fact that he is an exceptional athlete helped, but it wasn't the only reason he was having so much success. Nick didn't overcomplicate the extremely complex chess match that is BJJ. He approached it realistically. He knew his limitations and where he actually had an advantage over most people *because* he had only one leg. It was incredible to watch this trial-and-error process take place. He got to a point where he was choking far more experienced grapplers uncon-scious in training what seemed like at least once a month. It was time to promote him. Nick was a blue belt, meaning that he had around three or four years of consistent training. The next belt up is purple, and he was more than overdue. So he showed up to practice one day and we put him through an excruciating hour of nonstop fighting with multiple people and various weapons to the point where he had noth-ing left. We stood him up, took his blue belt off, and tied a purple one around his waist. I remember looking around at the other students and seeing the disbelief in their faces—not because they didn't think he could do it, but because they couldn't believe *how* he did it, how he improvised certain positions and techniques to benefit him even when completely exhausted. It was simple, but genius to watch.

When I saw Nick pass his final physical assessment to earn his place back on his ODA and successfully complete multiple deploy-ments after he left the combatives committee, I wasn't surprised. No one around him was. We knew that anything he set as his goal he would not only accomplish, but crush.

Though I was one of Nick's coaches in BJJ, he actually taught me a lot more than I taught him: how to be a better coach, a smarter competitor, a better athlete, and an overall more disciplined person. No matter how big an obstacle in front of me seems, I think back to the mindset and execution that I saw Nick adopt to get back to his profession as an operator on a team. I seize the motivation to accom-plish my own mission. Love you, bro.

Trey Pace
US Army

From left to right: Nick, Trey, Jason, Josh, Tim

Purple belt promotion, Team R.O.C., October 6, 2016

FOCUS

Focus:

1. a center of activity, attraction, or attention
2. directed attention (*Merriam-Webster*)

To remain disciplined, we must remain focused. This right here is essential. We have our plan. It is broken down into a series of objectives. Each objective has a series of requirements/tasks that we must accomplish to reach objective secure. We know there will be a host of challenges and obstacles along the way. We anticipate setbacks. We project failures. We are prepared. But what are we actually focusing on during the process? The reality of it is, it is our choice.

There is a lot out there regarding positive mental attitude (PMA). Yes, I agree positive thoughts are contagious and put us in a much better place than negativity. My fear with this, however, is getting stuck here—relying too much on it, expecting positivity alone to create results. This is, of course, incorrect. We must remain practical. Therefore, I prefer a slightly modified PMA—productive mental attitude.

Oftentimes the mission can seem daunting. Most of our dreams are big. We dream big, and why not? After all, life isn't a dress rehearsal. The problem with pursuing big dreams is, quite frankly, the sheer size. How am I supposed to actually do this? Sure, I have my plan, but damn, this is huge. The answer: focus.

Our focus will typically begin with our objective. That is the short-term goal we are currently working toward. It is among our first thoughts every single morning. So right there, we are scaling down the mission to something more manageable. From there, we shift again downward to the task at hand, the task that falls in line with objective secure. A single task. Something completely manageable. That task is the focus.

It is like trying to build a bridge a mile long. From where we are, the only way we can see the other side is through a set of binoculars. And even then, it is tough to see, but we know it's there. If we spend too much time focusing on the entire bridge, the dangers associated with its construction, the hazards we will have to face, the likelihood of success can be too much to handle (stress). But what if we focus entirely on the single component we are working on? One single piece.

I know this rod needs to be connected to that joint. That is the task. To do that, I need eight bolts, eight nuts, eight washers, a wrench, and pliers. I gather my tools, meticulously lay them out dress right dress,[56] triple-check that I have everything I need, and then get to work. I grab a single bolt, a single nut, a single washer, and my tools and begin attaching the rod to the joint. One turn after another, focused, watching the threads to ensure they are not crossed. First bolt complete. Then to the second. Focused. Same execution. Then the third and fourth until all eight are secured. I stand back and check the rod. It's locked in. Task complete.

The focus at no time was on the bridge. The focus was to connect this one component as perfectly as it can possibly be assembled. Then on to the next component (task) with the same focus. Repeat. Repeat. Repeat. Obstacle. Setback. Interruption. Repeat. Repeat. Repeat. Finally your bridge is complete. I refer to this as microfocus. And it is what I recommend ninety-nine percent of the time.

But why ninety-nine percent of the time? Why not one hundred percent? When we are driven, more often than not, this focus is manageable and enough to get going. Again, we know this is a requirement. There will come times, however, as discussed, when this is not working. Even though I need to accomplish this task, the justifications and excuses are coming in too strongly and I simply do not have what it takes to put in the work. Now is where we fall into the one percent. Now is where we shift our focus. We shift to what is waiting for us at the other end of the bridge.

If the objective I am working toward is, say, to get a promotion at work, the task at hand is to get into work thirty minutes early every day so I can make fifteen extra calls. Unfortunately, at this moment, I just cannot seem to be able to get myself going. I am unable to microfocus on the task because the current objective just isn't reason enough

---

56 Military terminology used when organizing a formation of individuals or a plethora of equipment.

to move. Okay, fine. The promotion suddenly seems irrelevant. I begin to rationalize why, perhaps creating an entirely new course of action right in that moment, one that doesn't require me to do anything right now. Shift.

Focus on the house you want to build for your family. The dream home you and your spouse designed together. The home that will put your children into a better school district. The home that is in a safer environment. The home that you and your family can comfortably live in together while creating millions of happy memories. That is the mission. That is what is waiting for you at the other end of the bridge. Is that enough to get you out of bed? Is that enough to deal with your boss? The answer is yes. More than likely it is. If it is not, I would proceed directly to Phase 1. Perhaps this isn't the mission after all.

SPRING 2015. Prior to earning approval to return to my detachment, I had to undergo a series of tests and assessments to determine my ability to perform on operational status. My command put me through the ringer: a variety of physical evaluations, proficiency evaluations, and even a psychological evaluation (more to follow on this one). For approximately ninety days, I was examined under a microscope, and for good reason. There was a lot of concern with putting an above-the-knee amputee back onto a detachment that was set to deploy back to Afghanistan conducting kinetic combat operations. Nobody had a previous example to compare me to. Yes, plenty of amputees had remained on active duty. A handful of below-the-knee amputees had returned to combat. But an above-the-knee amputee doing the same was something nobody was aware of having been done before. Tensions were high. At the end of the day, our commander would be the one assuming the risk. God forbid something happened to me or, even worse, to one of my teammates as a result of me being there, and he would have some difficult explaining to do. I understood that. Therefore, I was okay with whatever they wanted me to execute.

Following my last physical evaluation, I was given the green light to return. Around two months later, in the summer of 2015, I was back in Afghanistan, exactly where I wanted to be. And although I had to perform just about every physical exercise there is as part of my evaluation, I quickly realized I had a lot yet to learn.

Our team began conducting operations immediately upon arrival. And I do mean immediately. As soon as our flight came to a stop on the tarmac, the Special Operations Task Force (SOTF) command team boarded the plane to talk with our detachment leadership. A developing situation required our immediate intervention. The game was on.

I was held off the task org[57] for several of our initial operations—ones that were determined to be the most physically challenging, typically determined by the terrain within the operational area. Although I had made it back to the team and back to Afghanistan, we all knew I had a lot of work left to do. It drove me insane. Yes, I was incorporated into the majority of operations. But each time I was not, I was filled with rage. Nobody wants to sit on the sidelines, particularly when the boys are rolling out onto something that is likely to get nasty. That became my mission. Get out on operations—all operations.

The terrain, the heat, and the OPTEMPO[58] are just a few of the variables I did not or could not replicate during my training stateside. I needed time to acclimate. It was time to get to work.

---

57 List of personnel participating in an event.

58 Operational tempo: the pace at which we work, oftentimes dictated by the frequency of operations being conducted.

I laid out my plan. I had so many tasks I needed to perfect that it seemed impossible. Couple that with the overarching concern of being a liability on the battlefield. That weighed on me tremendously. I made an oath to myself, my family, and my teammates that I absolutely refused to be a liability. I was either an asset or I wouldn't be there. Period. I was convinced the only way to know was to get myself to a point where we all felt confident with me on the task org. That would be accomplished through work—a metric ton of work.

I didn't focus on the bridge. At times I would focus on the mission, the goal at the end of the bridge—being included in all operations—but ninety-nine percent of the time I was focused solely on the task at hand. Early mornings, late nights, when the boys were resting or reading or watching movies, I was training. At every opportunity, in between everything else we were doing, I was training on these tasks, the gaps I found in my game, one component at a time.

I can recall one of the more frustrating tasks was getting into and out of a Mine Resistant Ambush Protected (MRAP) All-Terrain Vehicle, a.k.a. MATV.[59] To get into and out of these trucks, one must climb up around four feet with the use of a couple of metal steps. As with most military vehicles, the MATV is designed for function, not comfort or accessibility. Of course, getting into and out of one of these was simple as a two-legged dude, but in 2015, it was anything but. To say this was frustrating would be an understatement. This was also something I did not even consider during my train up to get back onto the team. But it was a challenge nonetheless.

I began drilling over and over again. In and out. Trying different foot placements. Different hand placement. How I shifted my weight. Then I did the same with kit on. Then with a rifle. Over and over and

---

59   An acronym within an acronym—classic military vernacular right there.

over again. I had a teammate videotape my reps so I could watch the tape and check for deficiencies or wasted movement. I had them put me on a stopwatch. Over and over. I checked my time against one of my teammates to compare. I focused solely on the task at hand. I wasn't thinking about all the other tasks (components) I needed to master, and I certainly wasn't thinking about the bridge. Just this one piece of the puzzle. Focus. Rep after rep until I felt it was sufficient.

I repeated this process throughout the entire deployment, even after I had displayed enough capability to my leadership where they felt confident in putting me on more and more operations. The bridge was built. It was shaky and it needed additional attention, but I had made it across.

SUCCESS IS THE SUM OF small efforts performed daily. Little things become great accomplishments. We must gain and maintain control of our focus. Meditation, prayer, yoga—a variety of tools are available to assist. Find what works (research) and engage (execute). Doing whatever it takes oftentimes includes things we wouldn't have even considered incorporating.

HARD WORK

Now that we chose to stay on track, it's time put in the work. Here is where the tangible gains are made. Bottom line up front (BLUF)—good things come to those who work hard. Great things, however, come to those who are willing to do whatever it takes, to those who are willing to push themselves to a higher level.

JULY 2014. I was fortunate to be assigned to the SOCP committee as an instructor. Not only was I passionate about combatives and BJJ, but it is a physical job, which I saw only as additional training opportunities. I knew full well what I was going to have to put myself through if I was to have a legitimate shot at getting back onto the detachment. I was going to have to push through pain, ignore fear, sacrifice every irrelevant aspect of my life, and work harder than I ever had to in the past. I was going to have to go through hell.

I can recall a conversation I had with Toni (my girlfriend at the time), explaining that I was going to have to lock myself into a dungeon filled with discipline, focus, and determination. One where my life revolved around eating, training, and sleeping. Any and all distractions were to be eliminated. I was on a mission, and I desperately needed her support. She understood.

And so it began.

Legend:

Cal = Calories

P = Protein

C = Carbohydrates

F = Fats

BCAAs = Branched-chain amino acids

0400: Wake up

0410–0440: Rehab, stretching, range of motion, calisthenics, yoga

0445: Meal One (shake)

Whey protein: P: 26 g, C: 0 g, F: 1 g, 113 Cal

Greens (negligible)

½ cup fresh berries: P: 1 g, C: 11 g, F: 0 g, 46 Cal

0450: Shower and change for the gym

0530: Meal Two

Two cups (dry) oatmeal: P: 20 g, C: 108 g, F: 12 g, 620 Cal

Two cups egg whites: P: 48 g, C: 0 g, F: 0 g, 192 Cal

0600–0730: Strength training

BCAAs: 7 g

Creatine: 5 g

0730: Meal Three (shake)

Two cups egg whites: P: 485 g, C: 0 g, F: 0 g, 192 Cal

One cup prebaked sweet potato: P: 2 g, C: 27 g, F: 0 g, 117 Cal

One cup frozen berries: P: 2 g, C: 30 g, F: 1 g, 137 Cal

8 oz. pomegranate juice: P: 1 g, C: 36 g, F: 0 g, 148 Cal

0735: Shower, change for work, administrative tasks (emails, class rosters, etc.)

0900–1030: Teach whatever class was on the schedule

1035: Meal Four

8 oz. chicken: P: 67 g, C: 0 g, F: 15 g, 403 Cal

One cup (dry) brown rice: P: 15 g, C: 143 g, F: 5 g, 677 Cal

1040–1130: Finish teaching morning block of instruction

1130: Students go on lunch break

1145–1245: Myself and the other SOCP instructors go to 82nd Airborne Division fight house for BJJ/MMA open mat (no instruction, just show up and grapple)
   BCAAs: 7 g

1250: Meal Five (shake)
   Whey protein: P: 26 g, C: 0 g, F: 1 g, 113 Cal
   One cup (dry) oatmeal: P: 10 g, C: 54 g, F: 6 g, 310 Cal
   ½ cup fresh berries: P: 1 g, C: 11 g, F: 0 g, 46 Cal

1300–1530: Teach afternoon block of instruction
   16 oz. coffee, black

1545: Meal Six
   8 oz. ground beef/ground turkey blend: P: 49 g, C: 0 g, F: 34 g, 502 Cal
   One cup (dry) brown rice: P: 15 g, C: 143 g, F: 5 g, 677 Cal

1600–1700: Administrative tasks, shower, change for training

1730–1900: Team R.O.C. (local civilian MMA/BJJ gym) for BJJ/MMA practice OR the gym for endurance training
   BCAAs: 7 g
   Creatine: 5 g

1905: Meal Seven (shake)

Two cups egg whites: P: 48 g, C: 0 g, F: 0 g, 192 Cal

One cup prebaked sweet potato: P: 2 g, C: 27 g, F: 0 g, 117 Cal

One cup frozen berries: P: 2 g, C: 30 g, F: 1 g, 137 Cal

8 oz. pomegranate juice: P: 1 g, C: 36 g, F: 0 g, 148 Cal

1930: Home, shower, laundry, dishes, study, read, spend time with Toni and our dogs

2100: Meal Eight

Eight whole eggs: P: 48 g, C: 3 g, F: 38 g, 543 Cal

½ cup almonds: P: 10 g, C: 10 g, F: 23 g, 287 Cal

½ cup walnuts: P: 15 g, C: 6 g, F: 37 g, 417 Cal

Veggies (negligible)

2130: Sleep

Repeat

Daily Macronutrient Totals: P: 456, C: 674, F: 179, 6,135 Cal

Daily Macronutrient Percentages: P: 30%, C: 44%, F: 26%

Daily Water Consumption: 1.5 gallons

THIS MAY SEEM EXCESSIVE. Excessive protein, excessive calories, excessively regimented. What is important to consider is the frequency and intensity with which I was training. My body needed the fuel, and I needed work in a lot of areas. However, I freely admit that during this time frame I was somewhat out of my mind. I was obsessed with reaching my goal. This became apparent to most people around me, and although I was never told directly, I am positive this was the reasoning for the psychological screening as part of my return to the ODA evaluation process. Every day, I was all in. Relentless.

My training program was developed with input from our unit's strength and conditioning specialists, our dieticians, my fitness "consigliere" Paul Newt, my physical therapists Kelly and Tara, and my personal experience. It was highly sophisticated and complex. It had to be, given the variety of areas in which I required progress. The next challenge was the execution.

I was accustomed to hard work prior to losing my leg. I attended Boston College High School as a kid, predominantly because of its football program, which also carries an extremely challenging academic program. I played football at the collegiate level and managed to grind out my bachelor's degree. I was the honor graduate of the SFQC. Upon arrival to my first ODA, I did not have a senior bravo as a mentor.[60] Those are just a handful of examples, all requiring hard work. But I did not truly know what hard work was until I arrived at this stage of life.

Yes, the physical output was extreme. I was annihilating myself daily. But at least equally challenging was the focus and discipline. I knew I needed to crush myself in the gym, on the mats, and on the track. But I also knew that without the proper nutrition and rest, this would be impossible. The constant preparation was exhausting in itself, particularly my meals as I am not a fan of cooking. In fact, to say I cook would be disrespectful to the term. I essentially sanitize food

---

60   The standard ODA is a twelve-man team comprising a captain, warrant officer, team sergeant, intelligence sergeant, and two of each of the remaining MOSs (jobs): weapons sergeants, engineer sergeants, communications sergeants, and medical sergeants. This typically allows for a "senior" to be paired up with a "junior" within these MOSs.

so it won't kill me when I eat it. But I had to cook two to three times a week to have my fuel ready to go. I also had to take care of things like showering, dishes, laundry, and having all the necessary clothing to accommodate my daily activities. It all took its toll. It was constant.

These may seem like odd things to pose such a mental challenge. It may sound simple. And the truth is, it is simple. What made it difficult was the monotony, day in and day out. Actually, the physical training, as brutal as it was, was the highlight that was the reward. It is while we rest that the effects of the training happen—the nutrition-facilitated adaptation. However, during training is when we can feel the process. Our muscles enlarge from the weights, the sweat pours from our bodies, our hearts pound, our lungs burn. We are provided immediate feedback that tells us we are making progress. The remaining tasks do not offer the same. But they must get done. It's the monotonous, simple requirements that are oftentimes too difficult to maintain. The constant preparation with zero immediate effect. We must trust the process. We must remain disciplined.

Both physically and mentally, I pushed beyond what I knew was possible. I reached a degree of persistence and physical output I did not know existed. I truly walked the line between determination and madness.

In my heart of hearts, I know it is possible for people to find this level without having to get their leg shot off by a machine gun or experiencing some other sort of traumatic event. For me, that is what it took. But it was there the entire time. Losing my leg was simply the catalyst. With that came a fire for overcoming the adversity I faced, and I simply could not accept anything less than success.

The research was conducted. I was fortunate to have some truly elite professionals within the field to help me. Together we developed the plan. Now all that was left was the work. Miles and miles of hard work that only I could do. Yes, on some days I had people physically around me to support me, and yes, I had a list of people in my corner, but I was in a dungeon. I put myself there. It was me versus the pain. Me versus the fear. Me versus the naysayers and the doubters. It was me versus me.

HARD WORK DOES NOT GUARANTEE success, but without it there is a guarantee: the guarantee of defeat. Don't let that be you. Now is the time to go all out. Now is when we craft our ambition into reality.

NICK LAVERY DIET — Analysis

Compiled for: NICK LAVERY	Date: Jul-14	Height (in.): 77.5	BMI: 26	LBM: 202.9
By: PAUL NEWT	Age: 31	Weight (lbs): 223	BodyFat %: 9.0%	Fat Mass: 20.1

8 meals/day

0445 MEAL ONE

1 scoop(s) Whey Protein	76	0	1	113
0.5 cup, fresh blueberries	0.6	10.5	0.2	46
Greens (negligible)				
	27	11	1	159
	67%	26%	7%	100%

0530 MEAL TWO

2 cup 100% liquid egg white(s)	48	0	0	192
2 cup, dry, Quaker Oats, Old-Fashioned	20	108	12	620
	68	108	12	812
	33%	53%	13%	100%

0730 MEAL THREE (shake)

2 cup 100% liquid egg white(s)	48	0	0	192
1 cup(s), cubes, sweet potato	2.1	27	0.1	117
1 cup(s), frozen mixed berries	2	30	1	137.0
8 oz 100% POMegranate juice	1	36	0	148.0
	53.1	93	1.1	594
	36%	63%	2%	100%

1035 MEAL FOUR

8 oz chicken	67	0	15	403.0
1 cup(s) (dry) brown rice	15	143	5	677.0
	82	143	20	1080
	30%	53%	17%	100%

1250 MEAL FIVE (shake)

1 scoop(s) Whey Protein	76	0	1	113
0.5 cup, fresh blueberries	0.6	10.5	0.2	46
1 cup, dry, Quaker Oats, Old-Fashioned	10	54	6	310
	37	65	7	460
	31%	55%	14%	100%

1545 MEAL SIX

8 oz Ground Beef, Ground Turkey blend	49	0	34	502
1 cup(s) (dry) brown rice	15	143	5	677.0
	64	143	39	1179
	22%	49%	30%	100%

1905 MEAL SEVEN (shake)

2 cup 100% liquid egg white(s)	48	0	0	192
1 cup(s), cubes, sweet potato	2.1	27	0.1	117
1 cup(s), frozen mixed berries	2	30	1	137.0
8 oz 100% POMegranate juice	1	36	0	148.0
	53.1	93	1.1	594
	36%	63%	2%	100%

2100 MEAL EIGHT

8 whole eggs	48	3.1	37.6	541
0.5 cup(s) almonds	10.0	10.0	23.0	287
0.5 cup(s) walnuts	15.0	6.0	37.0	412
veggies (negligible)				
	73	19	98	1247
	23%	6%	70%	100%

Daily Totals:	456	674	179	6135
Daily Macro:	30%	44%	26%	100%

New Energy & Weight-loss Training Systems
Personal Training & Coaching Services
Coach Paul NEWT | web: paulnewt.com

THE WORDS OF PAUL NEWT

"He who has a why to live can bear almost any how." —
Friedrich Nietzsche

"Why?"

"How?"

I imagine Nick gets these questions frequently from people who do not know him well, whether they boldly fire these questions at him with a mix of incredulity and confusion shortly after meeting him, or politely wonder these questions in their own mind after discovering this man exists.

At the root of these questions is the attempt to comprehend where such a strong, inexhaustible internal drive comes from, and how the person asking can find that phenomenon for himself or herself. I am not sure I will be able to give you the answer you are looking for, but I will do my best to offer you advice from my perspective. My name is Paul Newt. I became friends with Nick in approximately 2004. Besides having common social interests at the time, Nick and I internally recognized that we shared many similar mental paradigms and life philosophies. The fact is, guys like Nick and me naturally gravitate to each other and others like us—guys who have that "fire." I actually call it "intense internal fire." We recognize this commonality quickly and quietly. It goes unspoken. There is an innate, subtle under-standing—an imperceptible nod. This quality landed Nick where he naturally belongs, among peers with that "fire in the belly," the same indomitable will, among our nation's elite military forces. Nick's life path has taken him far away from my immediate geographical circle and those great years we were able to partner up for training (and eating!), but he continues to pay me the great honor of acknowledging the depth and breadth of my knowledge and expertise in regard to strength training, conditioning, and recovery methods; various models of physical exercise; and nutrition, supplementation, and advanced dietary theory. He may believe that, without my guidance in regard to transforming his physique and radically improving his physical performance, he may have not ended up where he is. I do not believe that. Without Paul Newt, Nick would still have found a way. He would have found a way because that is the way he is built. Like the Terminator, he is a machine that absolutely will not stop. Nick's intense and inextinguishable internal drive is responsible for his success in overcoming challenges and adversity, and it allows him to continue to perform as the only above-the-knee amputee in military history to make a full return to his SF team.

I have spent a lifetime exploring the subject of the psychology of performance, an exploration that happened incidentally as a result of an absolute obsession that began for me at age twelve. My obsession was and continues to be how to achieve the perfect body, both in terms of performance and aesthetics, and how to be stronger. "Where the mind goes, the body follows," was one of my many early mantras, recognizing the power of the force of will. It occurs to me now that, although implicit in what I do, I do not consider the work I do with clients an endeavor of sports psychology, but rather a process of understanding man's ability to adapt physically, mentally, emotionally, and spiritually. Discovering and harnessing man's ability to adapt to stresses on all four of these "spheres of self" is what I do. I naturally focused first on the development of the physical self because it seemed the most obvious and accessible pathway to survive and thrive as a twelve-year-old boy who was being violently abused on a daily basis by a drug-dealing, deeply disturbed stepfather. As a current-day strength coach serving a variety of personal training clients, I still begin with the physical component of the process, which is, of course, necessitated by the expectations of the client. However, I will affect the client mentally, emotionally, and even spiritually, as a natural part of the coach-student relationship over time. And, based on my experience, I have learned that high achievement does require the training and harmonizing of all four spheres of self.

I can talk all day about training, eating, and recovery methods. In fact, most days, I *do* talk all day about training, eating, and recovery methods. The most important thing I possess at this point in my career is my experience. I celebrated my forty-ninth birthday in 2020. I sometimes joke with my clients that, "I have wasted my life in the gym so you don't have to." The second most important thing I possess is my internal drive. It's technically the most important. Without an intense and seemingly inexhaustible internal drive, I never would have gotten started. I never would have had the endurance to continue to grind out backbreaking, sometimes soul-crushing workouts over almost the past four decades, despite a nearly crippling back injury at the end of the 1990s, despite almost dying three times, despite triple bypass surgery. Without this piece of me that refuses to submit, refuses to kneel, refuses to quit, I would have never accumulated a now vast level of experience. Much like Nick, the intense internal drive is what gets everything started. I cannot speak for Nick, but my "fire" comes from a dark place filled with grief, shame, and hate caused by childhood trauma. Fire, as an element, both figuratively and metaphorically, has the power to help your life or to take it from you. Mine has done some of both. Contemplating whether someone can accomplish great things in life without "fire" is a frequent debate in my mind. I am sure a form of this question has come up in several conversations with Nick over the years. "Can a highly successful person draw great levels of intensity from peace, joy, and happiness, rather than from unresolved anger and rage?" I am constantly looking for real-world examples.

The reality is, I do not believe I have accomplished enough (yet) to hold myself up to Nick for comparison, but we do seem to share similar internal drives and similar notions of how the world is supposed to work. Nick and I often arrive at the same training hypotheses, experiments, and solutions, even though we have not partnered up for daily workouts for over a decade or more, and we sometimes go extended periods of time without "talking shop." Nick is the embodiment of a hero, and this once student of mine has become a master. What he has accomplished personally and professionally has come back to inspire me. He has exceeded any expectation I could have imagined for him, he is now a master on many levels, and he continues to grow. I feel honored to have been part of his journey, but I feel small next to Nick, literally and figuratively. One of the several benefits of being friends with Nick is having a similar mind to compare notes with and ease anxieties I may be experiencing. Many times I feel a sense of relief about certain negative thoughts I am having *after* I compare notes with Nick and discover he is thinking exactly the same things, oftentimes with even more ferocity than my already radically polarized perspective.

An example that comes to mind is when we talk about PRs at the gym. PRs are personal records. Just as it sounds, it is a note you make of breaking through to a new level of performance. Personal records are always bittersweet for us, because on one hand, there is a momentary feeling of exhilaration and accomplishment. Then those positive feelings quickly fade for guys like me and Nick and are quickly replaced with internal dialog like, *Why aren't you doing more? Why are you still so weak?* and, even more severe, *You're a joke. You are failing to achieve your goals. You are running out of time.* Let me describe an actual event that I still remember vividly, even though it happened decades ago. I always do an exercise called bent-legged dead lifts (BLDL) at the end of leg day. Basically, I *trash* my legs, then after about ninety minutes of squats and squat-type exercises, before I go home, I perform the BLDL using something I call my "20/10/1 Methodology." Based on previous dead lift days, my set of twenty on this particular day in 1993 was to be set at 405 (four forty-five-pound plates on each end of a forty-five-pound Olympic bar). After I did a fairly easy 405 pounds times twenty repetitions, I was supposed to do 585 pounds (six forty-five-pound plates each end) for two to six reps. Well, I got two only reps at 585 pounds, and I was immediately disappointed and angry with myself. Even though the day was a PR, I felt like I had failed for not being stronger. *What am I doing wrong?* I asked myself. *You've been lifting for ten years* (I was twenty-two years old), *and that's all you can do? You're pathetic. You better figure out how to do better next time.* Without even asking him, I know Nick can likely describe a similar experience he has had in the gym.

Speaking of the gym, at the end of day, the reason you are reading this book is to take something from it that you can use—at least, that's the reason I hope you are reading. So, aside from the mental/emotional/spiritual factors, what does Nick do in a physical training sense that allows him to do the things he does in the real world?

The simple answer is that he uses systems of training, eating, and biological recovery that encourage his body to perform at or above the level necessary for the fulfillment of his varied military job roles. It is important to add that Nick is working toward an extremely high level of performance in his own mind that he views as "acceptable" and that *exceeds* anything the military would demand of him. As you might guess, the details of these systems are sophisticated and complex, but elegant. I can give you an idea of the necessary framework, but the details of Nick's specific systems are for him to disclose and relate.

When I think of physical training, I think of *strength* training. Without strength, you have nothing. Strength is the cornerstone of every physical event, even long-distance running. Developing strength requires consideration of the various types of strength, reflective of the energy systems of the body, and the neurological demand of each type—explosive strength, speed strength, absolute strength, relative strength, and muscular endurance. Since I mentioned it, let's talk about running for a moment, because although it is an extremely basic exercise modality, it is perennially misunderstood. First, let's get something straight. The vast majority of you are *too weak* to use running as an effective *training* modality. What you are actually doing when you are running is *testing*. And you fail this exam in a variety of ways: shin splints; knee, hip, lower back, or even neck problems and/ or pain; or obesity. Yes, running for most of you is actually making you *fatter* because you are unqualified to use this form of exercise productively. Long story short, your relative strength, how strong you are in relation to how much you weigh, is the critical factor. Why do 150-pound men tend to excel in running competitions? Well, because when you are a male and you weigh only 150 pounds, it is really easy to get to a double bodyweight squat (loading twice your bodyweight on an Olympic barbell and squatting ass to the grass). It's real easy to do twenty dead hang pullups. It's real easy to do fifty consecutive dips. Running performance is a function of relative strength. The stronger you are, the faster you run, at the same bodyweight. Period. Again, without strength, you have nothing.

Real-world example? One of the best runners I know is squatting almost two and a half times his bodyweight. A real ass-to-the-grass squat, not that half-squat, "parallel" squat version. An "Olympic" squat. At 180 pounds, this ex-speed skater is squatting 430 pounds.

But you know what? He runs even better at about 165 pounds, at the same strength level–obviously.

For those of you looking to follow in Nick's footsteps in regard to military service, this is valuable information. But for those of you just trying to get in the best shape of your life or to achieve the highest possible levels of performance, it is equally important. Understanding how running fits into a training program is just an important as the strength training system you may be using.

The training system I use personally is a system I have nicknamed "4 PoiNTS." The P, N, T, and S stand for Paul Newt's Training Split (or System). The "o" and "i" stand for "output" and "input," respectively. The number 4 is because this is a four-day split routine, meaning the entire body is addressed via four distinct training days. The number 4 also refers to the four physical qualities I am training at all times: speed, strength, muscular endurance, and mobility (flexibility). The number 4 is also a tip of the hat to my personal blog, theperfect105.com, and the four components of the self–the physical, mental, emotional, and spiritual components of self that must be in harmony for success in any endeavor. Nick's personal training program is an adaptation of 4 PoiNTS, modified for his specific needs, but congruent in theory and application. For the sake of brevity, I would like to provide an outline of seven fundamentals that are critical to the success of any training program.

1. Find opportunity in what appears to be a setback. This is a big one. I often say things like, "If you break your arm, look at it as an opportunity to train your legs." Think about all that training time you can stop wasting on your upper body and that now you can dedicate toward getting super strong in the squat! This type of attitude will help you to not only

survive the inevitable crises that lie on your horizon but also to achieve what might initially seem impossible.

2. Become excited about the end goal by imagining how you will feel when you reach it. In Nick's case, *envisioning* becoming the only SF above-the-knee amputee in military history to return to combat was critical to him making it a reality. I remember reading in one of Arnold's books where he described how he would continually visualize and experience vividly in his own mind how his victory would feel *before and during his process of getting there.* "Where the mind goes, the body follows."

3. Be consistent. Understand that low-volume training systems are wishful thinking sold to inherently lazy people. The most successful athletes usually work out somewhere in the range of fourteen to twenty-one sessions per week. The name of the game is "how many productive, constructive workouts can you implement and recover from (per unit time)?" When preparing Olympic athletes, a training year is divided into four thirteen-week periods. An Olympic training cycle of four years is therefore sixteen, thirteen-week periods. That's it. If you complete four hundred constructive training workouts, and your competitor completes only two hundred constructive training workouts, who do you think is more likely to win the day of your event? If I had a nickel for every article I've ever read emphasizing dog shit like, "You only grow when you rest" and "How to avoid overtraining," I'd be a rich man. Most of you need *more workouts*, not more rest. Stop rationalizing that an "off day"

is "probably needed" on days you are just being lazy and probably recovering from nothing more than the Irish flu.

4. Install a logical program design. Training (and eating) follows the laws of math, physics, and chemistry. Programming that violates these laws yields extremely lackluster results. One important example I can give you is in regard to the organization of training and exercise sequencing. *Important*: The training order is dictated by the central nervous system demand. Would you attempt a one-, three-, five-, or even ten-rep max in the squat *after* running a quick mile? Many blunder in this way or in ways similar to it. For effective training to occur, whatever has the highest central nervous system demand must go first. Because strength is essentially measured in time, looking at the duration of the event will help you place each exercise event in the right spot. Think about how long a three-rep max in the squat takes to perform. About ten seconds? Now think about how much time it may take you to run a mile (as fast as you can). Seven minutes? Ten minutes?

5. Understand the difference between training and testing. As I mentioned briefly when talking about running, there is a difference between training and testing. There is a state of flow, a feeling of being in the "zone" when training, a euphoric state when your output is very high but your feelings of stress are very low or even nonexistent. The "trick" of training, if there is one, is to perform very high workloads while minimizing any negative stress. Training must be constructive, not destructive.

6. Do not waste valuable training time on unproductive and/ or irrelevant exercises. If seventy-five to ninety minutes is all you have for your main workout of the day, you don't waste a single minute of that valuable training time on silly exercises like tricep kickbacks or one-legged stiff-legged deadlifts on a Bosu Ball, or the latest super-creative exercise of the day you saw on Instagram. If you have all the training time in the world, sure. Waste your time on crap like that. But if you want to maximize your return on investment (ROI), pick exercises that are specific to what you need to improve and that have high value. High value, or high ROI, means you are receiving a tangible effect from the exercise. An example would be rotating in safety bar squats with a low box on the max squat day. On your next squat day, your chosen squat feels lighter and you hit a PR. Safety bar squats off the low box are likely a high-value exercise for you at this point in time.

7. Figure out where you are weak and improve it! It's easy and often satisfying to go to the gym and do what you are good at. However, the real gold to be mined at the gym is discovering what you suck at and improve it. The caveat to this would be to not waste time improving something that has zero affinity with your goals. This process can be greatly facilitated if you have the good fortune to be training with a team interested in the same specific type of high performance. An obvious example would be if you are a shot putter and training with a team of shot putters and you discover that your teammate who throws two meters farther than you is using twenty kilograms (forty-four pounds) more than you on the incline barbell press. Obviously, your solution may lie in improving your incline press. If you train by yourself, answers can be more elusive, and you will need to engage in a continual process of discovery and experimentation to figure out what you need to improve to meet your goals. But that's what it's all about.

As I stated, my personal program and Nick's personal program are extremely similar. Both programs include the same core elements and pay respect to the seven fundamentals outlined above. How we both plug in all these factors to the microcycle, mesocycle, and macrocycle is decided by prioritizing short-, medium-, and long-term goals. This necessitates the optimization of the microcycle and the systematic manipulation of training variables over a predetermined period (mesocycle, macrocycle)—a.k.a. periodization. For example, my microcycle is a six-day repeating sequence of days, optimized for my goals. It is much more common to use a seven-day microcycle because it is directly compatible with the standard seven-day workweek. Since having my weekends free from work does not really matter to me, a six-day microcycle is fine. For periodization, I employ what I call an integrated periodization model. To summarize, it means that instead of separating my development phases into mesocycles (i.e., thirteen-week phases), I am integrating more than one training objective within the microcycle. By carefully placing each training objective within my six-day microcycle, I am able to do multiple types of physical development.

Getting back to Nick's specific training program, although similar in theory and core elements to mine, he has tailored the arrangement and details to his specific goals. What makes this fun, interesting, and rewarding is comparing notes and seeing what works and what fails under both our systems. Because we can "speak the same language" to each other, we can utilize each other's data, compare notes, and accelerate learning.

These days, Nick and I both have demanding schedules, and the more demands we self-impose, the greater the necessity to organize everything into an efficient, productive plan and maintain the discipline to execute our efforts with the highest standards. It is the comprehensiveness of the plan, combined with the discipline and an intense force of will, that have allowed Nick to do what he has done and continue to do what he does. The machine does not stop.[61]

Paul Newt
Master personal trainer / Fitness consigliere

STRUCTURE

Structure:

1. something arranged in a definite pattern of organization (*Merriam-Webster*)

Our daily schedule informs us what we are doing and when. This is, of course, created based on many of the *Objective Secure* considerations and requirements. And like any schedule, this provides us with some structure—a guide. Simple right? Yes, it is. Just keep this in mind:

(1) Our structure increases our efficiency. Greater detail minimizes the likelihood of wasted time or energy. What we are striving for is

---

61 I realize there is a lot of material here on physical training. I asked Paul to dive a bit deep into his methodologies based on the volume of questions I frequently receive on fitness.

economy of motion—the process of minimizing unnecessary physical and perceptual stressors. No wasted movements. We can find these principles in business, in martial arts, and throughout everyday life.

FROM THE INSTANT I STRAP ON MY PROSTHETIC, a clock begins to tick. It is only a matter of time until I must take it off. Perhaps simply to wipe down my liner and leg of the built-up sweat, or perhaps I need to let my stump rest for a while due to significant wear and tear. Either way, it is inevitable.

When not on my prosthetic, I have three options to be mobile: hopping, crutches, and a wheelchair. I can feel Kelly's[62] blood boiling with even the thought of my hopping around. Refraining from doing this was one of the first lessons I learned. For one, the chance of falling is high. If and when that happens, the fall is likely to be catastrophic. Additionally, hopping can cause an injury, either traumatic or gradually, particularly in the knee. Being completely aware of the dangers and having the utmost respect for Kelly, I do hop around for extremely short distances on occasion, typically in the gym when conducting single-leg training.

Crutches are my preferred legless method of mobility. While I enjoy the extra physical training value, crutches are easily thrown into the back of my truck and I'm out. The downsides of crutches include, again, the chance of falling, particularly on wet surfaces. I will never forget a spill I took at a Bethesda, Maryland, grocery store. Long story short, it was pouring rain, I had been using crutches frequently and my confidence in them was high, so I was bombing

---

62 My Walter Reed physical therapist.

through the parking lot. I came whipping through the automatic doors and the second I hit the linoleum floors, my crutches slipped out from underneath me. It was a disaster. My crutches went flying, along with the bag I was carrying. Hell, I think my shoe may have flown off. Thankfully, only my ego was hurt. Aside from the physical risk, the problem with crutches is the inability to use my hands while moving. This drives me nuts.

Last is a wheelchair. I use a chair in my home, and really that's it. It is simply a hassle to transport. I am fortunate to have a sound leg that provides alternate means of mobility. My leg also allows me to move in a chair without the use of my hands by pulling myself across the floor. Now I can move and use my hands simultaneously, something that comes in handy (dad joke).

I am undoubtedly my most functional when on my prosthetic. Not only did I spend the first thirty years of my life with two legs, I spend most of my time since losing my leg on two legs as well. Here I am as efficient as possible. But the clock is ticking.

Many variables determine how fast the clock ticks. The weather, nutrition, terrain, type of activity, intensity of activity, etc. Sometimes I can go an entire day without needing to take off my leg; other times it's within an hour. I learned that while on two legs, I need to maximize my production. Every step brings me closer to needing to take it off, so I need to minimize wasted movements.

This desire for maximum efficiency has at times gotten a little extreme. If/when I forget something in the house after getting to my truck, for example, I become far angrier with myself than warranted. Wasted time, wasted energy—not economy of motion. These things, of course, happen, but there is value in specific attempts to minimize their occurrence, even simply storing my everyday items (phone, wallet, keys, etc.) in the same place every day.

The desire for efficiency also assists with discipline. On a typical day, when I get home, I want to get my prosthetic off ASAP. Odds are, I had two to three physical training sessions on top of whatever training we did for work that day, and my stump is beat up. And while I have yet to find a task I am unable to do on crutches or in a chair, all will take longer and be more difficult on one leg.

I have yet to live in a home with adaptive modifications. A variety of options are available to facilitate these upgrades, something I will certainly tap into at some point, but for now, I simply don't need them. Furthermore, I have concerns with becoming reliant on these enhancements. The world is not ADA (Americans with Disabilities Act) compliant, especially the areas of the world where I spend considerable time. As far as I am concerned, I have an obligation to remain conditioned to the world as it is. Austere environments do not adapt to you; you adapt to them. Odds are the mud hut we are living in somewhere in the Middle East or Africa or wherever is not going to have a gradual slope ramp leading to the main entrance or showers with the dimensions necessary to accommodate a wheelchair. Living within a home built with two-legged occupants in mind keeps me prepared for my living conditions when it's time to go to work. That, or I am simply a stubborn SOB.

Regardless of how tired or sore I am, when I walk in, I have work to do. If my family is home and awake, I, of course, address them first. Then its game time. Dishes, laundry, take the trash out—whatever I need to get done. I handle my chores as required, not because I want to and not even because I need to. Yes, I need to get the work done, but I could do them on one leg. So why not just do that? Because efficiency matters. It's not just about getting the task(s) accomplished; it's about accomplishing the tasks efficiently.

---

(2) LIFE IS GOING TO GET IN THE WAY. Things happen. We are going to get knocked off track. The greatest plan ever created will almost certainly require adaptation or adjustment.

No plan survives first contact—an expression meaning as soon as you are engaged by the enemy, the plan changes. We spend considerable time war gaming and developing contingencies for these very circumstances. Regardless, we are forced to think on our feet and make quick decisions. We assess, analyze, develop new plans on the spot, and execute. So why bother planning at all? Because it gives everybody something to return to. A baseline with locations, times, procedures, etc. Things everybody knows so when able to get back on track, back to the plan, everybody knows what to do.

The key is to get back on track ASAP. Spoiler alert: Monday is not the only day of the week when we can get to or back to business. Let everybody else do that. We are going to take advantage of this habitual behavior and get back at it now.

When developing a schedule, I recommend starting with thirty-minute time blocks (i.e., thirty minutes, sixty minutes, ninety minutes, etc.). Mathematically, this comes easily. Additionally, it's strategic. When you come across a task that you know with absolute certainty will take only twenty minutes, just round up to thirty for planning purposes. Adding in a buffer for the unknown is sound practice. So what do you do when it actually takes only twenty minutes? Get started on the next task. What if the next task doesn't start yet, like a meeting? Reinvest that ten. Make some progress on something else. Read an article. Get in a quick stretch. Or maybe just relax. Reflect. Refocus.

COST OF AMBITION

Ambition:
1. an ardent desire for rank, fame, or power
2. a desire for activity or exertion (*Merriam-Webster*)

Ambition comes with costs. Some of these costs are obvious and things we have already discussed: sacrifice, hard work, discomfort, failures, late nights, and early mornings. Another cost—one less obvious and less discussed—is social.

Now we can quickly disregard those who genuinely don't want to see us succeed. They are irrelevant, so there is no associated cost. The "haters" of the world suffer from insecurity, they lack confidence, they look to tear down somebody rather than build themselves up, because it's easier. They are weak. Ignore and move on. Easy.

Now those close to us, the people who love us, the people we love and care for—these people matter. Regardless of the relationship, some may not understand what we are doing and why we are doing it, or perhaps they simply do not support it. This has a cost, and this is something we must forecast and be prepared to manage. Reasons for this lack of support and/or understanding include:

1. TIME
Our loved ones want our time because they love us. In the onset, they are genuinely supportive of the goal—cheering us on, helping in any way possible. Then the realization sets in that in order to accomplish this mission, we are going to have to prioritize the tasks necessary to reach the objectives along the way. This takes time—time that is spent elsewhere. A few weeks, even a few months, of this may be a

nonissue; however, as we know, consistency is essential, and eventually the diminished time together takes a toll. It compounds, leaving your loved one(s) feeling ignored or neglected.

Recommendation:

The easy button answer to this is simple: balance. However, this is anything but simple. The unfortunate reality is we can be in only one place at one time. Additionally, if everything is a priority, then nothing is a priority. Now we can have our priorities-of-life list that is constant. For me, that is family, profession, training, education, and recreation, the five pillars that make up my life. Through this lens, nothing is ever more important to me than my family. From the macro perspective, this is accurate. From the micro perspective, not so much.

> When my team and I are deployed, and we load trucks to move toward our objective, I am one hundred percent focused on the task at hand. In that moment, nothing is more important. When I am in the gym and I get myself underneath the barbell for a set of squats, I am focused entirely on the lift. In that moment, I am not concerned with anything else. Priorities shift minute to minute. The perfect balance does not exist. It is impossible to give every important aspect in life equal attention at all times, and it is equally impossible to progress in these aspects without focus and dedication. If everything is a priority, then nothing is a priority.

Perfect balance is an unobtainable goal. It is like being fast enough for a sprinter, or strong enough for a powerlifter, or smart enough for a scientist. The pursuit is never-ending, and we know it will never happen. But we continue striving for it regardless. How?

Time prioritization. In the military, the term "white space" has a few meanings, one of which is a block of time without a previously scheduled task or event. We must strive to eliminate as much white space as possible to increase efficiency.

If family is number one in our macro priorities of life, we cannot solely dedicate the remaining time we have left *after* putting in work on everything else. Same as accumulating wealth: we must pay ourselves *first*. And the same focus we have when getting on the gun truck or getting under the barbell we must have when spending time with loved ones. Put down the phone. Focus on the task at hand. In that moment, nothing is more important.

2. FEAR

They don't want to see us disappointed. "Manage your expectations." "Don't get your hopes up." It is out of love. Big goals are inherently a long shot. We have accepted the fact that there will be failures along the way. We have accepted the fact that it is going to be painful. For our loved ones, this is considerably more difficult to accept.

> *During my time at Walter Reed, there were times I was in constant pain. There were times when I was completely helpless. I couldn't clean myself, feed myself, nothing. My family had a front row seat for it all. Yes, it was difficult for me. I am warrior, a problem solver, an elite athlete, somebody who answers the call. Physically and psychology, being this dependent was brutal, but it pales in comparison to the difficulties my family was forced to deal with.*

> *I made my intentions clear from the beginning. Although my family obviously knows me well, even they did not think what I*

was striving for was possible. This allowed them to be support-
ive while remaining scared—scared that I just wouldn't quit,
and that in the process, I would destroy my body and my mind.

The thought of our pain and struggle may be too much for our loved ones to handle.

Recommendation:

Communicate our mission and intent. The mission is the 5 Ws (who, what, where, when, and why). Short, concise, to the point, in a single sentence. The intent goes into a bit more detail. This comprises the expanded purpose, key tasks, and desired end state. The expanded purpose is the explanation of how the mission is nested within the larger picture. Here is the opportunity to explain how the accomplishment of this goal coincides with our collective goals. The key tasks are our objectives—things that must get accomplished to accomplish the mission. We know this already; however, communicating to our loved ones will prepare them for what is about to happen. Last is the desired end state—simply framing the future environment once the mission is complete. Where will we be, what has changed, who has been positively impacted? Our passion, thoroughness, and attention to detail will show and supersede their fear.

3. RESENTMENT

Resentment:

1. a feeling of indignant displeasure or persistent ill will at something regarded as a wrong, insult, or injury (*Merriam-Webster*)

Our dedication and progression make them feel bad about themselves. When a unit is assigned a task, everybody[63] works until the task is complete. This is ingrained into every service member from the very beginning. If individuals finish their specific task and look up and see others still working, they are moving to assist or find something else that needs to get done. The motivation to get the task completed as soon as possible in order to proceed to something enjoyable is present; however, there is also the psychological response: if they are working, so am I.

When those around us see our drive, our work ethic, or our dedication, they too may feel obligated to perform. Oftentimes, this is a positive chain reaction, accepted with gratitude and resulting in output. This may also, however, have a negative response. It is not a catalyst for performance. They cannot or refuse to reciprocate, which results in a feeling of laziness or lack of ambition.

Similarly, some have also attempted to achieve a goal themselves and were defeated. Our success will affirm their inability to do the same. In both cases, rather than being a source of motivation, we can become a source of resentment.

We must also be aware of the flip side of this same coin. When our ambition and determination are not reciprocated by those around us, our loved ones, it can result in *our* resentment toward *them*.

Recommendation:

Make them part of the process. If the mission is to get in shape, make it a family event. Everybody joins the gym, goes together, competes against each other. If the mission is academic, ask whomever to quiz you or proofread your paper. If the mission is professional, ask

---

63 Minus the shammers.

whomever to QCQA your slide deck, rehearse your sales pitch to them for feedback, ask for a recommendation on what to wear for that important pitch meeting. With this, we are limited only by our imagination and effort. At the end of the day, the advice or assistance or output may be worthless, but that is not the point. The entire goal is involvement. Remember: we are stronger as a unit.

Additionally, we must recognize that people grow on their own terms and according to their own timelines. We can attempt to present the example, we can aspire to motivate, but we absolutely cannot force others to want to improve themselves. Look at this like chopping down a tree, perhaps with a hatchet. With each swing, we are making progress, however slow it may be. We may want the tree to fall over immediately. I mean, how can this thing not just *want* to fall over right now?! Trees can be extremely thick, they can have deep roots, and some trees have been standing in that exact spot for years. It may not be that simple to just fall over.

Remember, *we* are the ones who have decided to make a change. It is *our* responsibility to do what we can to communicate our intent and purpose. It is *our* responsibility to create a team dynamic. We cannot assume those around us will immediately strive to do the same. Be patient. That does not mean simply sit back and wait. Do the work, which in this case extends beyond reps in the gym, pages in a book, and hours at the office.

We are going to make mistakes. We are going to mismanage our time. This will almost certainly affect those around us whom we care for. Perfect balance does not exist. That's okay. Expect it, and then learn from it. This process, although painful, increases efficiency. We learn where we can afford to spend less time and also discover opportunities throughout the day or week when we can increase productivity, both with our loved ones and with regard to our mission.

4. COMMUNITY

Community:

1. a unified body of individuals
2. a group of people with a common characteristic or interest living together within a larger society
3. a group linked by a common policy (*Merriam-Webster*)

Last, and probably the most difficult in terms of the social cost of ambition, is who we surround ourselves with, our community. Some quantify this in statistical terms as it relates to the law of averages, stating we are the average of the five people we spend the most time with. This is a convenient way to predict income, athletic ability, intellect, etc. While from a mathematical perspective, this is not exactly accurate, from a conceptual perspective, it is spot on. The old expression "birds of a feather flock together" means those with similar character, background, or taste tend to associate with one another. Sociology tells us this is accurate. To put it bluntly, if we hang around with losers, we will become a loser.

THE MEDICAL EVALUATION BOARD (MEB) is the process to determine if a service member does or does not meet the medical retention standards following an injury or situation in which a physician determines an MEB necessary. The MEB documents the medical condition and duty limitations of the service member, at which point, when necessary, the service member is referred to a Physical Evaluation Board (PEB) to determine the severity and impact of the situation and ultimately whether the service member can remain in service.

August 2014. A month after returning to my unit at Fort Bragg, my MEB was initiated. Of course, this process begins with a brief that explains the MEB process. From the moment the brief ended, I redefined MEB. To me it was the Military Eviction Board—a process to remove service members from the Army. My mindset at that time was one hundred percent focused on getting back to my profession. I couldn't hear anything other than that. Placing considerable emphasis on the transition process out of the military is understandable given the number of MEB cases and the statistical result. Couple that with the fact that many (if not most) service members going through an MEB want to be separated from service. We are all products of our environment. I can look back and understand it. That said, when somebody walks in with an obvious burning desire to remain in, a shift in focus is warranted.

As part of the MEB, service members are assigned a Physical Evaluation Board liaison officer (PEBLO), an individual to quarterback them through the process. Countless appointments and documents require the service member's attention. The PEBLO assists in managing these requirements. My first PEBLO—let's call him Stan—did not shift his focus. I was in the "eviction board" process. I recognized it immediately, and I forecasted the inevitable friction.

In Stan's defense, my goals seemed unattainable. The duty description and physical requirements for an SF weapons sergeant are intimidating for most able-bodied people. Here I was, sitting in Stan's office, seventeen months after getting my leg shot off by a machine gun, telling him that I would be able to do all these things. I only needed a little bit of time. This did not compute in Stan's mind. Despite the repeated pronouncements of my intentions, his focus was on my disability benefits and medical care, and what he perceived as my certain transition to life as a civilian. This wasn't going to work for me.

During one appointment with Stan following a brutal training session, I lost it. In hindsight, I may have still been a bit wired from the caffeine. I wasn't exactly yelling, but I was making my point heard. Turned out it was heard by everybody in the office. I not so calmly explained that I needed a PEBLO who was on the same sheet of music as me. I needed somebody who understood my goal and was willing to work with me to achieve it. I paused my not-so-professional rant once I noticed the gathering of additional staff around me, including the supervisor of the office—let's call him Brad.

Brad asked me to join him in his office. We sat down. I was still wound up tight, breathing heavily, sweating, fists clenched. Brad could obviously tell I was upset. He just sat there, giving me a moment to get my bearings, before asking, "So, how is your day going?" with a smile. My first instinct was to blast him directly in the face. A split second later, I realized what he was doing, relaxed, and just laughed. I apologized for the not-so-eloquent outburst. Brad told me it was no problem, to forget about it, and to explain to him the problem. I made my intentions clear. I stated I did not feel Stan was comprehending what I was doing. I needed a PEBLO who got it, somebody I could work with. Otherwise, I'd handle the process on my own.

I, of course, had no clue how this would be received. I was confident that firing a PEBLO was uncommon, to say the least, and I was prepared for the "Well, he is your assigned PEBLO and that's it" response. But that's not what happened. Brad did some scrolling through his computer screen before telling me he was assigning me a new PEBLO, "Rachel." He told me Rachel was familiar with working with SF guys, which said all that needed to be said. He told me to follow him, and we left his office.

As we turned the corner into Rachel's cubical, I knew I had found my teammate. Rachel's entire aura screamed motivated, deliberate, and aggressive, and as if that wasn't enough, she had an SF crest pinned to the wall of her workstation.

"Rachel, this is Nick. I am passing him off to you. Nick is with 3rd Special Forces Group and is determined to return to his unit."

Rachel turned off the music that was quietly playing (AC/DC, if I recall), looked up, and said, "So you're the one making all this racket? Take a seat. Let's get you back to work." Problem solved.

OUR COMMUNITY IS INCREDIBLY INFLUENTIAL on us. If we surround ourselves with people who lack ambition, people who are overly dependent, people who are constantly making excuses, they will systematically drain the energy from even those with the strongest will to succeed. There will likely come a time when we must remove these energy drainers from our lives in exchange for those on the same page as us, or better yet, those on the same page but further along—those better than us.

If we run a one-hundred-meter sprint with a group of people who are slower than we are, we will win. Every single time, barring something crazy, we will win. If we run the same sprint with people faster than us, we will likely lose, but our time will be faster. Running with those faster than us, better than us, will force us to dig in just a little bit deeper and strive just a little bit harder. We may continue to lose, but we will become faster; we will become better.

Dropping Stan for Rachel was easy. I had no emotional ties whatsoever. It was strictly business. This, however, is not always the case. There are "influencers" out there who describe cutting people from our lives almost as easy, as if it is a no-brainer. Some of these influencers go so far as to include one's parents or spouse. To paraphrase: "If they aren't on board, cut them loose." I feel, in some situations, with some relationships, this isn't quite so simple. Hence, my emphasis on involvement and communication with those we love and care for. Unfortunately, despite our best efforts, this may not be possible. We may come to a crossroad, a decision point. We may have to decide between maintaining the relationship or pursuing the mission. The type, length, and strength of the relationship will determine just how challenging this decision will be. I cannot tell you the answer. Nobody can. A sacrifice will be made one way or another. I will say only this: I spoke on resentment. This is a powerful feeling. We must ask ourselves, *If I never reach mission success so I can maintain a relationship with this individual, will I resent that person forever? And if so, what durability and quality will our relationship have?*

We may not be able to change the people around us, but we can change the people around us. Yes, you read that correctly. It simply means, despite our greatest efforts, we may not have an impact. "You can lead a horse to water, but you can't make him drink." At the end of the day, we can make people smile, we can make them laugh, we can make them feel good, but whether or not they are happy is completely and utterly out of our control. The same applies to ambition. So, while we may be unsuccessful with our attempts to be a spark for positive change within another, we always have the option to surround ourselves with others.

Perhaps the relationship is salvageable. Perhaps it will just take work that we are willing to put in. Or maybe we need to move on. Regardless, we must seek to surround ourselves with people who push us, who challenge us. People who are also striving for success. We need the community tripod.

MENTORS: Those we learn from. Those we respect. Those we look to emulate. Fortunately, with advancements in technology,

192 | OBJECTIVE SECURE

our mentors are no longer limited to those within our geographical location.

ALLIES: Those to grind alongside of. Those also striving, not necessarily toward the same objective or mission, but striving nonetheless. They, too, are unstoppable and unreasonable. Our allies provide support *and* competition. They boost us up while also seeking to win. This is our team.

PROTÉGÉS: Those we teach. Those we influence. Those looking up to us. Mentors and allies are people we can identify almost immediately. Protégés, on the other hand, we must earn. In order to advise, we must live the life. We need the experience. Earning a protégé in itself is a goal, something to strive for, because once we have that relationship, it raises the bar even further. It pushes our capacity. Earning the ability to teach takes work. Teaching enhances our ability. As our ability increases, so does our span of influence. It is cyclical.

Despite our greatest efforts to communicate, involve, and choose our community, the ambitious will remain misunderstood by most. Because even those who get it, those right there with us, those who fully and deeply support us, are not able to one hundred percent completely understand it. They can't see the vision as clearly as we do because it's ours. This is not selfish or inconsiderate. We have an obligation to ourselves. Only we are able to identify who we want to be, and most of us have aspirations, even if they are buried way deep down inside, of greatness. It is *our* mission, *our* journey, and only *we* can turn that vision into a reality. So regardless, figuratively and/or literally, we will do many things alone. Fear not—there is much to gain in this solitude.

It is easy to work hard when the lights are on, when our family or our friends or our teammates or our boss or even our haters are watching. We want to do well. We want to make them proud or show them what we are made of. Our pride drives us to put out. The problem is, these individuals are not always going to be there.

———————

MAY 2019. With about three weeks left in the warrant course, I was told what team I would be joining—a dive team.

Dive teams, even if only through anecdotal evidence, are high-performing teams, and this is due to one reason. Dive School arguably is the most physically and mentally challenging school in the US Army, if not the entire military, where human beings, land-living mammals, are forced to function without our most essential resource: oxygen. Those who graduate to earn the coveted Dive Bubble insignia reserved solely for combat divers have successfully demonstrated the ability to force themselves through the most unnatural thing a human can do. This is accomplished through sheer will and the acceptance of death over defeat. When a single team is formed with individuals who have made it through this extremely fine filter, a powerful force is created—a dive team.

Upon hearing the news, I was immediately met with excitement. I wanted to be on a highly respected and highly requested team for operational employment. My immediate next thought was of Dive School. After graduation from the warrant course, I returned to Fort Campbell and sat down with both my company and battalion chain of command (CoC). I was congratulated on the successful completion of the course, formally told what team I would be joining, and then immediately told I was not expected to attend Dive School. My first thought was anger. "Yes, I obviously realize I have one leg, but to be on a dive team you must be a combat diver, and there will be no exception for me." They could sense my frustration. I was told the reason why I was going to this particular team was because it comprises a bunch of highly aggressive guys who require strong leadership. Any projection of weakness would result in an immediate lack of respect and an inability to perform the function of a leader. I understood what they were saying; we were, after all, talking about a dive team, who along with being solid performers, are also historically aggressive and at times borderline (if not completely) insubordinate—the type of detachments that drive command teams crazy, but are also the same teams they call on when in need of results.

I expressed my desire to attend Dive School. This was met with support; however, nobody knew if this was physically or administratively possible. That was on me to figure out.

Getting administrative approval is a story for another day. Let's just say, when it came to getting myself physically prepared, I knew I was going to have to push myself harder than ever before. Obviously, I was dealing with a distinct disadvantage, but I was positive that if my cardiovascular endurance, my breath hold, and my carbon dioxide (CO_2) tolerance were at high enough capacities, I could do it.

February 2020. With the help of my teammates, strength coaches, and dieticians, I got my program dialed in. It felt extremely similar to my train up to return to the ODA in 2015. It was going to be hard, extremely hard. It called for at least three training sessions per day and the fuel and sleep necessary to support the training. I once again sat down with Toni to explain that I needed to revisit the dungeon. She knew this conversation was coming. And although we were at an extremely stressful time in our lives (another story for another day), she was supportive. A lot had changed since the last time I went to this dark place during my train up to get back on the ODA. I was now on a detachment as the ADC, which meant I was already working long days, Toni was working hard and making monumental advancements in her career, and I was now a father to a three-year-old son. Despite these additional challenges, she picked up some of my slack to allow me the time I needed to prepare, train, and recover. My angel. Amazing. Into the dungeon I went. It was time to work.

My day started off as usual with my calisthenics and stretches. From there, I went into my CO_2 tables—a method of training to gradually increase the body's tolerance of CO_2. Important note for the future combat divers out there: The urge to breathe comes from a buildup of CO_2, not a lack of oxygen (O_2). The ability to hold one's breath while remaining static and with ample time to inhale and exhale prior is one thing. However, conducting breath holds repeatedly with nothing more than one or two breaths in between while also moving is something entirely different. CO_2 tables work as follows:

+ Determine a reasonable amount of time to hold your breath. This is typically somewhere around half the time of your current breath hold max. So if while completely rested, relaxed, and with ample time to "breath up,"[64] you can hold your breath for 2:00, you would set your breath hold time at 1:00 during CO_2 tables.

+ Each round you hold for 1:00 and begin with a rest time in between sets at 1:00. So a 1:00 hold followed by a 1:00 rest.

+ During the rest, you simply breathe normally. The goal here is to lower your heart rate as much as possible.

---

64   Deep inhales and exhales to open up the lungs.

✦ Round two, again hold for 1:00 followed now by a rest time of :50.

✦ Next rest period drops to :40, then :30, so on and so forth.

So while the hold time remains the same, the rest time decreases. It is amazing how even with the exact same amount of O2 in your lungs, the increase in CO2 makes it increasingly difficult to hold. When we breathe, we are expelling the built-up CO2 from the previous breath. The longer we hold, the more CO2 builds up. Restricting breathing during rest times prevents expelling the CO2 within the system, therefore increasing the discomforting urge to breathe.

This is quite a miserable way to start the day, which is also why it is beneficial. Knowing the additional inevitable pain that awaits throughout the hours to come, after CO2 tables, it is all downhill.

The remaining dry (out of the water) training sessions prioritized cardiovascular endurance with strength coming in as a secondary requirement. I specifically dropped all training protocols designed to produce size (hypertrophy). The goal was to be as strong as possible while also being as lean as possible. I needed to reduce the size of the machine in order to increase my cardiovascular endurance abilities.

On top of this, I was in the pool two or three times per week. My teammates and other SF combat divers facilitated my training. Every minute in the pool was brutal. These sessions consisted of training on the required events one must pass prior to being allowed to attend Dive School, as well as a series of "stress events"[65] that increase water endurance and that are events I would eventually experience during Dive School. The water is the ultimate equalizer. It will take the

---

65 A nice way to say torture.

biggest badass out there and turn him or her into a sniveling nine-year-old within minutes. This is, of course, understandable given that (1) the type of power needed to be strong in the water is truly trained only while in the water, a place that might as well be Jupiter to some, (2) it takes an exceptional level of endurance capacity to maintain through these training sessions, and (3) the fear of death, again, is a thing. After all, the body requires O2 above all else for survival.

My home gym is not robust, but it does have a couple of torture devices that proved to be essential: a rower in my garage and an assault bike on my back porch. It was at these locations that my mettle was tested. The standard home gym is not equipped the same as a training facility, typically due to two obvious factors: space and cost.[66] The upside of the home gym is convenience. It's right there. No commute, no waiting on equipment, no "best pop hits from the '90s."[67] There is also a subtle downside: convenience. No, that is not a typo. The hidden disadvantage is the same as the advantage. Because with convenience to train also comes the convenience to end the session early, the convenience for your family to interrupt with a "Hey, real quick...," the convenience to give a subpar effort without ridicule or judgment. And now is when I really confuse you. This brings opportunity.

You see, the training sessions during which I saw the most progress were done in my garage or on my back porch. These workouts were typically conducted at one of two times during the day: early morning or late night. It was just me, the darkness, some music, and the clock. My log maintained my performance (something we will discuss shortly), and it was during these sessions that I saw the most progress. Nobody cheering me on. None of my teammates or

---

66 Dwayne Johnson's Iron Paradise is anything but standard.

67 Unless that's what gets you going.

coaches there to lean on. Just me. Me versus me. Complete punishment. Torture. I'd end up on the ground, on my back, in pain, struggling for air. At times I asked myself why I was doing this to myself, only to answer my own question. Because it'll be worth it.

A quick story to paint the Dive Team and Combat Diver picture: Early 2015. The dive team in my company was precisely as described above. Our teams often trained and conducted operations together going back years. A good friend of mine—let's call him AB—was on that team, a combat diver to the core. AB and I went through the SFQC together. We were both weapons sergeants (18B); therefore, we consulted each other frequently.

Side note: when it came to the employment of mortars, AB was as surgical as they come. His abilities saved our asses during a Quick Response Force (QRF) operation in 2012, a story for another day.

Prior to 3rd Special Forces Group moving to the shiny new buildings it is in today, we worked out of these old, decrepit relics I am quite certain were built during World War II. Parking our personal vehicles was always a challenge. There just wasn't a lot of space within the immediate vicinity of the building. In the rear of the building was an area that had been designated to remain clear of personally owned vehicles.

AB was in a school at Fort Bragg; therefore, he did not come into the company building often. On one particular day, he did for one reason or another, during his lunch break. With little time to spare before needing to be back in class, he parked his car behind the building and ran inside. It took all of about three minutes for our company sergeant major (SGM) to notice. The SGM began screaming down the hallway, "Whose piece of shit hoopty is parked out back?!?!"

AB reluctantly came out of his team room to face the music. "It's mine, Sergeant Major."

I'll spare you the verbatim conversation and just say that the SGM came completely unglued. He raged, blood vessels popping in his forehead, Copenhagen flying from his mouth, as he screamed for a solid minute. Once satisfactorily purged, he turned and slammed back down the hallway like a pissed-off tyrannosaurus rex, guys from other ODAs bolting back into the confines of their team rooms after watching this glorious event transpire.

As the SGM reached his office, he began clutching his chest. With the sweat pouring from his now magenta-colored face, the SGM was having a heart attack. The B Team[68] medic laid him down on his office floor, grabbed some vitals, and determined he needed to get to the hospital immediately.

The insubordination of my brother AB nearly killed our company SGM. He was inevitably fine. It is a story we still look back on and laugh about. A reality of our profession is that the funniest stories are oftentimes events that came inches or moments from somebody's death.

WHEN WE PUSH HARD in these moments of solitude, we turn ourselves into our greatest adversary. We create a world in which nobody can push us as hard as we push ourselves. When we reach this point and get into this stride, we become invincible. From that point on, no instructor or boss or adversary can compete. They cannot induce the same degree of stress upon us as they can on others. We become bulletproof.

The willingness to work hard when nobody is there is not found within everybody equally, which is why these moments provide

---

68 Support team within the company.

opportunity. It is when nobody is watching, nobody is caring, when it's just you and your integrity, you and your desire, when you could easily give it fifty percent or not do it at all and nobody would know the difference. It is these moments when you push yourself anyway that tend to lead to the most progress. We must know in our heart that what we are pursuing is right. Yes, it is difficult and it can be lonely, but it's worth it.

CONSISTENCY

Consistency:

1. firmness of constitution or character (See *persistency*) (*Merriam-Webster*)

Unfortunately, it is easy to be great for a day. Anybody can do it. But it's the other 364 days that make the difference. And this is truly the most challenging aspect of execution—consistency.

A BODYBUILDER CAN BE DEFINED as a person who strengthens and enlarges the muscles of their body through strenuous exercise. Bodybuilding is the use of progressive resistance exercise to control and develop one's musculature for aesthetic purposes. An individual who engages in this activity is referred to as a bodybuilder.

Bodybuilding is an art. The goal is to form the human body a particular way, like a sculpture. The difference is a sculptor can simply add and remove clay as necessary to create the desired image. Bodybuilders must do the same; however, that comes only via consistent physical activity, proper nutrition, and an extremely disciplined lifestyle.

Competitive bodybuilding is a niche sport probably more accurately described as a cult sport. Bodybuilding competitions are not broadcast on major networks and do not make headlines[69] in the sports sections of our most popular publications. Although, with the expansion and accessibility of the internet as well as social media, the genre is growing in popularity, it is still and will likely remain in the background within the field of athletics. This is almost certainly why the term "bodybuilder" is used so interchangeably; whether an individual is competitive or not is irrelevant.

My training goals have been altered and modified over the years as my priorities have changed. At times, I have been one hundred percent focused on performance, with absolutely zero training intent toward the development of muscle mass (hypertrophy) or aesthetics.[70] Most of the time, however, there have been some training techniques and theories implemented with the specific purpose being to build muscle.

The same could be said with regard to my nutrition. At times, the intent has solely been to provide the necessary fuel to drive the training. That's it. Zero regard for aesthetics. Most of the time, however, my nutrition program is multipurpose. Not only am I seeking to adequately fuel my body to withstand the training necessary to perform, I am also cognizant of the image I see in the mirror.

Performance and perception of one's self—two things that are interconnected. Or as Hall of Fame wide receiver Jerry Rice put it: "Look good, feel good. Feel good, play good." But I have never been a competitive bodybuilder; in fact, at no point have I even referred to myself as

---

69   Or are even mentioned.

70   How the body looks.

a bodybuilder. Yes, I typically train with muscle development as a (not the) goal, and yes, my nutrition seeks to produce both performance and aesthetic results, but I do not consider myself a bodybuilder. I do, however, have an enormous respect for those who do.

Bodybuilders, and I am talking about those at the higher levels and those who look to achieve the higher levels of the industry, are among the most consistent and disciplined people on the planet. In order to achieve this goal, these people must live it. It is a 24/7, 365 commitment. Their meals, training, supplementation, sleep, stress, everything play a factor in their progress. For Arnold, Dorian, Ronnie, Jay, Phil, just to name a handful, it took years to get to their level of achievement. Day in and day out. Meticulous calculations, slight variable adjustments, ferocious training sessions. They had to continuously make sacrifices. A night out with their friends—nope. Travel to a destination wedding—nope. Explore other activities and hobbies—nope. Nothing else. All in. Yes, many also had/have families and were able to make it work. Most, if not all, also had to sacrifice relationships along the way that could have potentially become their families.

Whether or not this is a healthy lifestyle is something that can certainly be argued. Yes, there is the taboo side of the sport, that being drug use. Yes, it is surprising to read case studies that state some bodybuilders would gladly sacrifice a decade of their lives if it means they can become Mr. Olympia.[71] Fortunately, access to the information is available, and the risks associated with this lifestyle are being more accurately documented, researched, and disseminated today than ever even considered in years prior. As long as individuals understand these risks, they may choose the life they want to live. Skyscraper construction workers, deep-sea fishermen, loggers,

---

71   The Super Bowl of bodybuilding.

base jumpers, free solo climbers—there are a variety of occupations and hobbies that are inherently dangerous. Are these people crazy? Possibly, but the fact that they participate in such activities alone does not warrant a clinical diagnosis. They have a need to do these things, perhaps a passion for them. Who am I, or anybody for that matter, to judge them for what they choose to do? If you know the risks and choose to accept them, have at it.

An endless number of bodybuilders work out in every gym all around the world. Many, if not most, men have a desire to be muscular and strong,[72] something I am all for, by the way. Fitness is an enormous aspect of my life, and I would absolutely love to see more members of our society make it a higher priority within their own, even if solely for general health purposes. But there are very few elite bodybuilders. Sure, we can argue genetics and drug protocols all day, and both play a factor, but what is an absolute certainty is their commitment to consistency—the daily grind and continuous sacrifices. Most simply do not have what it takes to do it. This is something to be respected and something we can all learn from.

I spoke on monotony, how that is oftentimes the greatest challenge. It doesn't require an elite strength and conditioning coach. It doesn't require a dietician. It doesn't require facing death. It doesn't require being in an Ivy League school. It doesn't require people cheering you on. It doesn't require a fancy car, expensive clothes, or a huge house. It doesn't require followers or likes. What it requires is daily effort. It requires consistency.

---

72 Many women do as well.

DISCIPLINE, HARD WORK, AND CONSISTENCY. How can you stop someone who is willing to stay on track despite temptation, someone who is willing to sacrifice and put in the hard work, someone who is willing to dedicate himself or herself on a daily basis? How can you stop someone who is willing to do whatever it takes? The answer is, you can't.

PHASE 6. TRACK

THERE IS NO REASON TO OVERCOMPLICATE this one. It is simple. This is simply keeping track of what you are doing and how you are doing it. It's a diary, really, and for all my alpha tough guys out there, you will likely refer to this as a log. But that's all it is. We are logging our actions: what we are doing, how it's going, whatever. Now this can get as crazy and detailed as we choose. My logging started solely for my physical training, and the logs from the early 2000s are insanely detailed: every rep, every gram of food, every minute of sleep. One day was around three pages of data. Eventually I broadened the scope of my log to encompass more than training, and I only wish I had started that sooner because the same value it brings to training is the same value it brings to any other goal, or to life itself for that matter.

Now all information can be helpful, but what I found was, when I looked back, I was really looking at only a handful of data points. You will learn the same. I recommend going with what may eventually be considered overboard in the beginning. Over time, you will determine what data points matter to you the most when you look back. And while you are logging, remember this. Be honest. Lying to yourself makes precisely zero sense.

I BEGAN LOGGING, as most did back in the day, with a pen and a notebook. This is like the Blockbuster Video stores in the early 2000s. It's only a matter of time until it's dead. In today's world, just about everybody walks around with a computer in their pocket or strapped to their hip. Somehow, my original logs being destroyed by sweat and/or extremely difficult to read due to the pre-workout making it damn near impossible to write legibly wasn't enough at first. I was old school. Eventually I came around to accept the advancement of technology for what it is—convenient and efficient—and made the transition.

There are, of course, a variety of fitness apps on the market to use. Personally, I am not a fan of any. I think they are entirely overengineered. But that is neither here nor there. What's important is storing the data in whatever way works for you. I have been using Microsoft OneNote for years now. It is simple, effective, and easily linked to my home computer. Typically, Saturday is my day to "deep dive" into my log. I will open it up on my desktop, clean it up, organize it a bit, and then update my macro tracker, which is nothing more than a Microsoft Excel spreadsheet that summarizes progress/regression long-term. More importantly, it allocates time to reflect on the previous week and to take a detailed look back at the days or weeks prior. This is a method, not the method, but certainly one I recommend trialing yourselves.

8 NOV 20 - SH n Arms - H3

Sunday, November 8, 2020   4:30 AM

Alarm 0400
Up 0405

Body weight calisthenics

Warmup

Right wrist tweaked. Yesterday during low row. Idiot

Triset x2

Dbl OHP - 35/8, 45/8, 55/8, 65/8, 75/8
Sngl ohp - 85/6, 90/6 x3
SS
Hammer curl- 25/10, 35/10, 40/10, 50/10 x4

Sngl lat raise- 20/12, 25/12 x3
SS
Sngl OH Tri extension- 40/12, 45/12 x3

Dbl front raise - 30/10 x3
SS
Band reverse fly - Purple band/15 x3
SS
Internal reverse curl - 40/10 x3

Face pulls - 4x12
SS
Cable extension - 4x12

Cable row / Pushup / Plank Finisher

––––––––

Assault bike
Fartlek
4 min warmup (Speed 20)
5 min 20/10 sprint (25)
3 min steady
        Recovery time increasing

50 ab mat leg lifts
Flutter kicks 30 x4

––––––––––––––––––

Meals (high carb day)
1.5 cups oats, 1.5 cups egg whites
Shake
Chicken and rice
Ground beef / turkey and rice
Chicken and pasta, apple, Pb
Honeybeard shake
Meatloaf, sweet potato
6 Eggs

––––––––––––––––––

-Got OPI tomorrow, Not as prepared as I should be, failed to prioritize
-Last minute prep for deployment feels chaotic, but the boys are ready
-Everything with Vin looks good, we are blessed
-In the redzone with OS, LFG

Bed 2130

GLOSSARY

Top/Other Notebooks

+ Cardio: Track cardiovascular specific progress.

+ Program: Current and previous training program outlines for reference.

+ References: Physical training and nutrition references (e.g., tables, articles, etc.).

+ Data: Physical measurements (e.g., body weight, caliper measurements, etc.).

+ PR: Personal record.

+ Supps: Supplement type, quantity, and frequency.

+ Breath hold: O2 and CO2 training sessions.

Title

+ 8 NOV 20: Obviously, this is the date of the entry.

+ SH n Arms: Strength training was my shoulders-and-arms-focused day within the split, a.k.a. microcycle.

+ H3: I was on week three of my six-week, hypertrophy-focused phase within the program.

Wake Up
+ The time I set my alarm, and the time I physically got out of bed.

First Training Session
+ Bodyweight calisthenics. This may be a variety of training types, typically done fasted (without eating prior).

Strength Training
+ Warmup: A dynamic warmup prior to strength training.

+ Right wrist tweaked: I had re-aggravated a wrist injury the day prior. Obviously, I was not very impressed with myself about it.

+ Triset: Doing three exercises back-to-back-to-back without rest in between (one minute rest occurs between rounds) for two rounds (i.e., "x2").

+ Dbl OHP: Double overhead press, a.k.a. military press, using two dumbbells (one in each hand). First with thirty-five pounds for a set of eight reps, then forty-five pounds for a set of eight reps, and so on.

+ Sngl OHP: Single overhead press, using just one dumbbell in one hand at a time, then switch.

+ SS: Superset, meaning doing two exercises back-to-back without rest in between.

✦ Hammer Curl: A biceps exercise.

✦ Sngl Lat Raise: Single lateral raise, a side deltoid exercise.

✦ Sngl OH Tri Extension: A triceps exercise.

The rest I am sure you can figure out.

Endurance Training

✦ Assault Bike, Fartlek: A training method for endurance and/or speed.

Nutrition

✦ Meals: high carb day. I have been running a carbohydrate (carb) cycle for several months consisting of two days low/moderate carb intake followed by one day of high carb intake, then repeat. Note: I do not annotate my macronutrient profile here because I know the numbers and my protocol has been the same for a while. For those embarking on a new or modified fitness journey, I recommend tracking these details until they become second nature.

Notes

✦ I annotate these upon first getting in bed for the night prior to reading (usually).

Bed

✦ What time I physically got into the bed. On a good night, I'm asleep within thirty minutes.

PHASE 7. ASSESS

THIS IS WHERE WE ANALYZE the state of our situation and identify areas of progress, stagnation, and/or regression. There are several types of assessments—let's touch on three.

1. PERFORMANCE

What do the numbers say? Our log provides the data for our analysis. What are the metrics? What is my current two-mile run time? What have my grades been the past four months? How many calls on average have I been making at work? How do my sales look? These are statistics. As long as we are honest at the time of input, they do not lie. They provide one hundred percent objective information.

2. EXTERNAL

For this, we need somebody to hold us accountable—somebody who is consistently in our lives. Not necessarily by our side all day every day, but there needs to be regular contact. Additionally, this individual must be comfortable enough with us to give it to us straight. Our parents may not be the best option. Parents have a tendency to be subjective; they love us too much to provide accurate and, at times, harsh feedback. Whoever it is—a teammate, coach, family member, friend—what are they seeing? Be prepared for negative criticism. More often than not, it is here we learn the most.

THE AFTER-ACTION REVIEW (AAR) is a professional discussion of an event focused on performance in order to determine what happened, why it happened, and how to sustain strengths and improve weaknesses. We conduct AARs following every single training event. While the "sustains" (things we did well) are important, we really make our money when we get into the "improves" (things we did poorly).

Acceptance of improves varies from individual to individual. Some are more open to the criticism; others get defensive quickly. There are a variety of psychological factors for this I will forgo, but typically, senior individuals take this feedback well. For one, we are conditioned to the process, having gone through AARs throughout our careers. We have developed thick skin. Similarly, we have had the opportunity to see the advancement of addressing our improves, which in turn makes us better.

We need this thick skin if we are going to be able to leverage our external assessment. We must recognize it as the opportunity it is, cast our egos aside, and be honest with ourselves. This feedback is coming from somewhere. Whoever is providing it is seeing something. Respect it. This doesn't mean we must immediately go "all stop," but at a minimum let's annotate it. Perhaps now we will notice it ourselves moving forward. It's like buying a car or naming a child. Once we do, we see it everywhere. And here we were, thinking we were unique.

3. REFLECTIVE

How do you feel? Our log, if utilized as recommended, also provides us with this data which may be the most difficult to determine. Many of us, particularly the type A personalities, struggle with being honest about how we feel. No matter what, we are "good." Lord knows how many times I have been asked if I am okay, clearly showing indicators that something is wrong (hence the question), and my response was, "Nah, I'm good." Now there is absolutely a time and a place to drive on. If this is coming as a shock, then you clearly have not been paying attention to this point. I am not saying we quit the second we don't feel good. Not at all. I *am* saying, however, that this is valuable information to annotate.

Remaining honest with ourselves with regard to how we feel is critical. Yes, we are going to crush goals, but let's strive to do this in a healthy manner. It is also important to remember we are going to be more productive when we are enjoying what we are doing—something obvious that many of us can overlook. Let's put aside our ego for a second. After all, this information is for *us*.

The assessment phase facilitates determining where we are struggling. We are looking for where we are lagging. We are looking for glitches in the system. We *cannot*, however, do this immediately.

Systems take time to showcase their worth. The greatest plan in the world, executed with absolute precision, is not going to accurately project its capabilities within a week. There simply aren't enough data yet.

Each goal is different, and even with the exact same goal, each individual's system will be different. They must be. We are all different. We each respond to different stimuli differently; therefore, we each have different requirements. We each have a variety of different variables to consider with our system design. No two systems are identical. Hence, the assessment. Fine-tuning our system is a never-ending game of trial and error.

So how long do we remain within a plan prior to our assessment? Great question. Unfortunately, again due to the uniqueness of each, there isn't an exact answer common to all. I will say that most will require at least a month. In that time, we are likely to experience enough triumphs and setbacks to collect enough data for analysis.

Truth be told, we should be assessing our status constantly. With each log entry, we are going to conduct some reflection. This is not only natural; it is healthy. But trust the process. Here is where our patience must engage. Annotate the thoughts, even adjustments, you are certain will be necessary. Maintain the course. Assuming you aren't in some sort of danger, drive on and continue to compile data. This will only solidify variables that require adjustment.

ENJOY THE JOURNEY

It is also important to enjoy the journey just as much as the prize. In the military, although certainly not limited to that profession, we tend to be goal-oriented, and success is based primarily on effects. I am a firm believer in this mentality. At the end of the day, a tree is judged based on the fruit it bears, not its desire to bear fruit. We do need to produce results. However, we exist in the here and now. Life is a gift, and while we are driving toward an objective that is linked to a mission, I want to challenge you to concurrently enjoy the process as well.

THE MOST VALUABLE ASPECT from my log was not my deadlift PR. It was not how many grams of protein I was consuming. It was not how many hours I spent reading. It was how I felt. Oftentimes, it was just a few words, maybe a sentence or two, but the quick synopsis of how I was feeling at the end of each day.

There were times when I would be making insane progress. My numbers in the gym and on the track were improving. I was getting good grades in grad school. Things with my family were good. According to the numbers, I was on a solid trajectory. But then I would notice the last section of that day's entry: how I was feeling. And there would be a noticeable trend of "frustrated," "tired," "unmotivated," etc. How can that be? I am crushing life right now. What I determined to be the glitch was my constant, and I do mean constant, focus on goals. The thousands of tasks I had to complete daily were all a means to an end. Most required microfocus, but in the back of my mind, I knew they were tied to a larger goal. It was the accomplishment of the objective, the accomplishment of the mission, that would bring me happiness.

But there is a problem with that. I spoke on satisfaction—how it doesn't exist for the greats, how as soon as we reach objective secure, we are looking toward the next ridgeline. For those of us who operate in this fashion, and for those who look to dial in, get serious, and begin making substantial progress, we must be aware of a potential threat, that being our entire life going by, and although we may have a list of accomplishments or a bunch of stuff, we failed to enjoy the ride.

According to the laws of biology, physiology, and medicine, I should not be alive today. If a medical school teacher were to describe my circumstances in 2013 to a class and ask the mortality rate, the answer would be ninety-nine percent. An estimated five gunshot wounds to the legs[73] from a truck-mounted PKM machine gun from approximately fifteen feet away: shattered femur, lacerated scrotum, severed femoral artery, a pressure dressing and tourniquet administered by the patient while in a substantial state of shock, sixty to ninety minutes on the ground prior to MedEvac extraction, blood transfusion with the wrong/incompatible blood type. A mortality rate of ninety-nine percent may actually be conservative.

This experience has provided me with many gifts, one of which is an enhanced appreciation for life. On my worst day, I am able to look back and be reminded that I should not be here—that every day is truly a gift. Again, I believe it is possible for people to have this level of appreciation for being alive without coming face to face with death. For me, this is what it took. Since this incident, I have gotten married, had a son, and have another on the way. My family is the highlight of my life. My son(s) are my strongest reminder to remain grateful. If things had played out "the way they should have," they would not exist.

Happiness is an essential aspect of life. Some would argue it is the entire purpose of life. I do feel that happiness comes in the form of success, which can be derived through the methodology of Objective Secure. We must continue striving forward, no matter what, but we also must enjoy the journey just as much as the prize.

This enjoyment is not only critical to happiness; it is also an indicator of whether we are on the right path, if we are striving toward the right mission. Chances are, the things we determine must be done to reach Objective Secure and mission success are things we will have to continue doing once we have reached the far side of the

---

73 An estimated four rounds to the right and one to the left.

bridge. If the goal is to become a Green Beret, the physical training, the studying, and the discipline will remain a part of your lifestyle for as long as you continue the profession. If the goal is to become a scientist, or a schoolteacher, or a professional basketball player, the tasks identified as part of progressing toward these professions will remain. In fact, the demand is likely to increase once you get there. If the goal is to build a new house, the work put in to be able to afford it must continue once it becomes a home. If the goal is to lose fifty pounds of fat, the nutrition and activity it took to get there must be sustained. If the goal is to be a better parent, the sacrifices to do so must remain.

It is an ongoing process. It doesn't stop. Therefore, if we are unable to enjoy the process and the journey, chances are we will not enjoy the prize. Either that, or the prize will be short-lived. We may reach the far side of the bridge, we may reach mission success, but not for long. Will some things get easier on the back end? Perhaps. Some, though, will likely get harder. This is an opportunity to check ourselves. Are we really on the right mission? Are we being honest with ourselves? Who do we want to be?

My suggestion is to leverage our assessment through this lens as well. Enjoy the process. Even the moments that are tough bring value. Take a second to appreciate the lesson learned. Allow yourself the opportunity to look back in a week or month or year and see just how far you have come. Remain proud of your accomplishments while putting in the work. And if it turns out you are consistently miserable, perhaps you need to reassess.

"Learn to be thankful for what you already have, while you pursue all that you want." —Jim Rohn

EXPERIENCE VALUE

There is value in everything. There is a positive side of even our worst experiences. The glass is half full. With some experiences, however, it is impossible to see the upside within that moment in time. Whatever happened is just too painful, too heartbreaking. We can feel only the hurt. Our log helps with this as well.

AS A SPECIAL FORCES WEAPONS SERGEANT (MOS 18B, a.k.a. Bravos), base defense is my responsibility. Early into our 2012 deployment to Afghanistan, I recognized a significant problem. I woke up one morning and crawled out from underneath the collapsed clay structure I was sleeping beneath to find around two dozen Afghans walking throughout our camp, all carrying AK-47s. While I recognized some as the Afghan National Army Special Forces (ANASF) team we were partnered with, many I had never seen before.

Special Forces detachments work with indigenous personnel. This is what we do. But we also must establish SOPs for everybody's safety. Our camp did not have much force protection measure to leverage. The team we replaced had been at that site for only forty-eight hours prior to our arrival. It was raw, to say the least. It was my job, along with the other Bravos, to develop and enforce our base defense and security systems. We had a lot of work to do.

Eventually we established an inner perimeter using procured chain-link fence, four-by-fours, old HESCOs, sandbags, and whatever else we were able to find. We also established an outer perimeter, our physical barrier between us and the rest of Afghanistan. In between the outer and inner perimeters was our motor pool[74] and our storage for nonsensitive items. The SOP we established was that, prior to any operations, only the leadership of our partner force would come into the motor pool area to receive a mission brief. The rest would remain outside the wire.[75] The leadership would then relay this to their sections and we would roll.

Along with our ANASF team, who lived with us, we were also conducting operations with Afghan National Army (ANA), Afghan National Police (ANP), and Afghan Local Police (ALP) personnel. We trained and advised these units when not conducting operations, including hundreds of different individuals. Tracking individual personalities was next to impossible. We needed some standoff[76] in situations when we were most vulnerable, inside our MSS being one of them. Hence, the SOP. Our detachment commander explained our SOP to the partner force leadership, and it was followed without issue. Until it wasn't.

On March 11, 2013, we were set to conduct a routine operation. As always, our partner force gathered outside our camp. The leadership entered the wire to receive the mission brief, only this time a truck also drove in. I noticed immediately that it wasn't right. I was pissed. *Do I address this now?* I thought to myself. It seems obvious that the answer was emphatically in the affirmative. Why wouldn't I? The answer to that question is rapport. This is a tough balance and arguably the most critical factor for an ODA's success. Fostering and maintaining relationships are the keys when conducting part- nered operations. I decided to hold off. I would address this with

74   A parking lot.

75   Perimeter.

76   Distance between.

my detachment commander after, and he would address it with the partner force leadership. This was a decision I must live with for the rest of my life.

This truck was a Ford Ranger with a mounted PKM in the bed. This is the weapon that would moments later rip my body to shreds, drastically altering the rest of my life. But this result is not the reason for my regret. The loss of my leg is not why I spring up sweating in the middle of the night. Living the rest of my life as an amputee is not why I continue to reanalyze my decision-making process that day. Our detachment commander, Captain Andrew Pedersen Keel, our infantry uplift squad leader, Staff Sergeant Rex Schad, and our MWD (military working dog), Bak, were all killed in action as a result of my decision.

Captain Andrew Pedersen Keel

Staff Sergeant Rex Schad

MWD Bak

It took years to be able to look at this event and extract positive value. The pain was too great. I couldn't see past my anger and the disappointment with myself. I couldn't see past the faces of my brothers who paid the ultimate sacrifice. It took time. It took a lot of reflection. It was hard, but I owed them this effort so their deaths were not for nothing. Gradually, I was able to gather the lessons learned.

Internal security SOPs, partner force relationship dynamics, and John Boyd's "OODA Loop" cycle[77] are just a few examples of what was extracted. We used our experience to better educate ourselves and those around us in order to minimize the likelihood of a future similar tragedy. The loss of these men brought value to those who remain in the fight. How many lives have been saved because of

77   Observe, Orient, Decide, Act.

their sacrifice? *There is no way to ever know, but I am certain it is substantial.*

The insider attack (a.k.a. green on blue) on March 11, 2013, is considered to this day the most catastrophic insider attack since the start of the global war on terrorism. It is referenced in schools and training events throughout the SOF community. As painful as it remains, we have managed to pull the positive value from this tragedy. We must get better. We owe this to the fallen.

———

THE WORDS OF
HELEN KEISER-PEDERSEN

NICK SENT ME A FEW SECTIONS of the *Objective Secure* manuscript to provide context for my words. Reading his account of the day of the insider attack broke my heart. I had no idea Nick felt such self-blame for what happened that terrible, beautiful, bright blue morning. It caused me to retrieve and re-read the report of the investigation that followed the death of my son, Captain Andrew "PK" Pedersen-Keel.

After noticing the truck inside the wire, Nick's decision to hold off and address the situation later is a moment in time we can never erase or undo. For the warriors responsible for our protection, men of goodwill, prudence and balancing each second on mission are herculean tasks. There are always wolves in sheep's clothing, with betrayal as the worst sin of all, and impossible to prevent.

Similar to Nick, Andrew had a goal: to be the best for this team of warriors. Similar to Nick, Andrew wanted to be in the fight alongside great operators. Similar to Nick, Andrew cared about everyone in his command. Both Nick and Andrew are who they were made to be.

The second time Nick was wounded in action brought him to Bagram Airfield (BAF) for medical attention. This is where Andrew first met Nick, as he was serving as the Night Battle Commander. This position gave Andrew a close association with Nick's detachment, who they were, and what they needed as they were within the most hostile and dangerous area.

December 2012, Nick's team needed a new detachment commander following an ambush that resulted in several casualties. Andrew was assigned the task. In Andrew's phone call home to update me about his new and highly desired assignment, he remarked "Mom, I got a team!" and later "You don't have a thing to worry about." That is all he could really tell me. Later, I learned he was referring to Nick, who he had met prior.

After seeing many photos from Wardak, I began to feel like I knew the team a little bit. After seeing pictures of Nick on his first deployment after his amazing and miraculous recovery, I understood what my son meant for me to uniquely understand.

March 11, 2013 happened. We buried Andrew in Arlington on March 28, 2013. My husband and I visited Andrew's team at Walter Reed Hospital the very next day, March 29, 2013. Unprepared for the devastation of what we would see and who we would meet, I wanted to help but was helpless except for the power of prayer.

Having worked as a nurse in vascular surgery, I understood the gravity of Nick's right femoral artery wound and the subsequent amputation, and I worried. Here was this giant of a man, in a hospital bed that seemed too small for him, as sad as anyone could possibly be, and who needed everything to work favorably in order to heal his high, right-above-knee amputation.

Despite wanting to comfort him, I knew I couldn't, at least not yet. Seven and one-half years later, I have yet to meet Nick in person. We converse, I follow him on social media, and I have loved him through his recovery, achievements, marriage, birth of his son, promotions, TED Talks, interviews, and more.

Separately, but together, we have both grown stronger and experienced the grace of forgiveness. Andrew's death was not Nick's fault, nor the fault of anyone else. It was a time of war.

As Nick went on to his destiny, my husband and I found our way by creating APK Charities. We are in our seventh year, doing what Nick has done: forging a positive way forward. There is one iconic picture that we use to promote Andrew's legacy and charity. It is of him standing tall, proud, and happy on the roof of an abandoned Russian tank, high up on a mountain top. I have always loved this photo, one that Nick just so happened to take himself.

Andrew was philosophical in his approach to life, and perhaps his own mortality. He chose as his high school yearbook inscription under his senior year photo:

"Just surrender to the cycle of things,
Give yourself to the waves of the Great Change
Neither happy nor yet afraid.
And when it is time to go, then simply go
Without any unnecessary fuss."
— T'ao Ch'ien

Andrew left us that day; Rex and Bak were taken too. So many life-altering injuries. But Nick and many of his fellow Green Berets showed us how to keep on living and stay in the fight. Nick is a warrior through and through. He doesn't know how to stop, and his recovery, positivity, and relentless determination have helped us as Gold Star parents become warriors as well.

Helen Keiser-Pedersen
Mother of Captain Andrew ("PK") Pedersen-Keel

SOMETIMES IT TAKES WEEKS, MONTHS, or years to be able to recognize the positive value of a particular experience. Let's look at this through an example that is perhaps more relatable. You're an athlete and you sustain a knee injury during training or a competition. You are hopeful, and then you get the MRI results. It is a complete ACL tear. Boom. Life is over (or so it seems—perspective).

In that moment, chances are any positivity will be hollow, a façade. This is the worst thing that could have happened and nothing but fear, worry, anger, and stress is coursing through your body. Let's assume you stay on track.

Let's assume you follow the *Objective Secure* guidance. Let's fast-forward twelve months. You're back. Rehab did its job. Life is good. You look back through your log over the past year. Due to the injury, your exercise selection was altered and some new movements were added. You adjusted your nutrition. You modified your morning routine. You increased your rest. You added another activity. Through these changes, your log informs you of the benefits. You have been exposed to some things that otherwise you would have not experienced. You see the value in doing this or that. You decide to sustain some. Even though your knee is back to one hundred percent, you maintain some of the lifestyle modifications. You incorporate them into the new system. Fast-forward another six months. Gains are going through the roof. You feel great. You are more efficient. You are more durable. You are resilient. It is in *that* moment, now looking back eighteen months, that you can appreciate and be grateful for the injury. As terrible as it was then, look how far you have come because of it.

PHASE 8. REPEAT

HAS THE GOAL CHANGED? If the answer is yes, repeat the process. If the answer is no, repeat the process with specific and intentional adjustments based on the identified lags or deficiencies.

+ Are our Lines of Effort (LOE) good to go? Do we need to add another?

+ Move to research. What information do I need to adjust my approach?

+ Where are we with our objectives?

+ Do we have an additional decisive point (DP)?

+ Are our LOEs correlated?

Boom. Execute. Back to work. Move out.

Continue to gather data. Stay the course. Trust the process. We cannot make brash decisions. Odds are there are variables within our equation that are working. The only way to determine what is creating positive effects is through small, incremental adjustments over time. It's hard. This separates the average from the greats. If it were easy, everybody would do it. Repeat. Repeat. Repeat. This process *does not stop*. Focus. It is worth it.

CONCLUSION

Warfighting function:

1. a group of tasks and systems united by a common purpose that commanders use to accomplish missions and training objectives. They are the physical means tactical commanders use to execute operations. The purpose of warfighting functions is to provide intellectual organization for common critical capabilities to achieve desired effects. (ADP 3-0). See graph on next page.

In other words, a warfighting function is a bunch of things being done by a bunch of people, all working in harmony to achieve a specific result.

The Mission Command Warfighting Function is the related tasks and systems that develop and integrate those activities, enabling a commander to balance the *art* of command and the *science* of control in order to integrate the other warfighting functions. There is a reason it is located in the center of the rest. Mission Command is the nucleus. It links everything together. It is both physical and conceptual in nature. It is a tool, a system, a methodology.

If this sounds familiar, it's because we are also describing *Objective Secure*—the connectivity between the multiple systems we must leverage. And in case you haven't already acknowledged it, *you are the commander.*

Commander:

1. one in an official position of command or control (*Merriam-Webster*)

Objective Secure is a group of tasks and systems united by a common purpose that *you* use to accomplish missions and training objectives.

Objective Secure outlines the physical means that *you* use to execute operations.

The purpose of *Objective Secure* is to provide intellectual organization for common critical capabilities so *you* can achieve desired effects.

Objective Secure is the nucleus that integrates mindset and actions, enabling *you* to balance the art of command and the *science* of control.

Objective Secure is a philosophy—a way of thinking. It is a philosophy combined with tasks—physical acts executed within time and space.

Reaching Objective Secure is also part of the process. Like in a tactical setting, it marks a key point within the operation. It signifies progress. As we know, securing objectives enables us to continue moving forward. We need the foothold. We need the momentum. One Objective Secure after another is how we reach mission success.

You crave success. You desire greatness. Yes, because you are different from the rest. You weren't born to be average. Mediocre is unacceptable. You have something special within you. You have a vision of doing more, being more. And you have the ability to generate this into reality. You have the ability to become more than anybody could have ever imagined. You have the ability to live life on your terms. Set your own path. Leave the world in a better place than when you found it. You have the ability to create a legacy that will live through the ages. Yes, I am talking to *you*. How do I know this? Because this is an option for any and everybody.

Greatness is not predetermined, something reserved for the special few. Tom Brady may be the greatest example of this truth. I'm biased, you say, because I am from Boston and obviously a Pats fan. I can feel the eye rolls. Fair enough, so let's look at the numbers: Tom Brady played at Michigan University from 1996 to 1999 originally as the seventh quarterback on the roster. The seventh! He was a backup his first two seasons, threw just five passes in 1996 and a whopping fifteen in 1997. His third year, 1998, was finally Brady's chance to play as a starter. Brady's senior year, 1999, was rife with challenges as he battled for the starting job. Halfway through the season, Brady finally separated himself to become the full-time starter.

The National Football League (NFL) Scouting Combine is an annual week-long showcase where college football players perform physical and mental tests in front of NFL coaches, general managers, and scouts. It is a final chance for prospects to demonstrate their abilities prior to the NFL draft. Here is the scouting report for Tom Brady:

+ Poor build

+ Skinny

+ Lacks great physical stature and strength

+ Lacks mobility and ability to avoid the rush

+ Lacks a really strong arm

+ Can't drive the ball downfield

+ Does not throw a really tight spiral

✦ System-type player who can get exposed if forced to ad lib

✦ Gets knocked down easily

As if this wasn't bad enough, my man Tom ran a 5.28-second forty-yard dash. For those unfamiliar, this is lava slow, and by far the slowest among all active quarterbacks in the NFL today.

In the 2000 NFL draft, Tom ended up being drafted in the sixth round (out of seven total) by the New England Patriots. He was the 199th pick out of 254 total. To put this in perspective, those drafted in the sixth or seventh round rarely end up making the team's final roster.

In 2001, Brady took over as quarterback for the Patriots midgame when Drew Bledsoe suffered a devastating injury, a historic moment propelling Tom Brady to where he is today:

✦ The oldest active player in the NFL (forty-four years old)

✦ Played in ten Super Bowls, winning seven, both of which are the most of any player in NFL history

✦ Earned a record five Super Bowl Most Valuable Player (MVP) awards and three NFL MVP awards

Among many other notable accolades, Brady has also been selected to fourteen Pro Bowls, which ties the NFL record for most selections. For regular season and postseason combined, Brady is first all-time in career passing yards and touchdown passes. He is one of only two players in NFL history to amass seventy thousand passing yards and one thousand rushing yards and is second in all-time in career touchdown passes. He is first in postseason career completions, passing yards, and passing touchdowns. He is the only quarterback in NFL history named to two all-decade teams and is one of only ten quarterbacks selected to the NFL 100th Anniversary All-Time Team.

The debate regarding the greatest quarterback or the greatest NFL player of all time is one that will continue forever. Regardless of the stats, this will remain subjective and open to opinion. I am sure you can guess where my vote lies, but the point is this: Tom was not a football prodigy from birth. His greatness was not a forgone conclusion. In fact, he was hanging on by a thread or flat-out cast aside by just about everybody. Meanwhile, nobody could see what he was doing, even though it was in plain view.

Tom's focus was unbreakable. His dedication to his craft boosted his understanding of the game to the highest level. He studied football constantly; therefore, he was the smartest player on the field. His training, his nutrition, his sleep all were meticulously regimented and executed with precision. Tom believed in himself, regardless of who around him did the same. He didn't care what people said. He couldn't hear it. He focused, he sacrificed, he worked, and when the opportunity presented itself, he was ready and struck hard.

I can relate to Tom, and most of you can as well, believe it or not. Am I a millionaire Hall of Fame quarterback? No. Am I in the conversation as the greatest anything of all time? No. In fact, I have never been the greatest at anything ever in my life. There has always been someone smarter, faster, stronger, more charismatic, more disciplined, funnier—the list goes on indefinitely. I struggled as a child. I struggled as a teenager. I struggled as an amputee. Few people believed I could do what I set my sights on, and I don't blame them. But like Tom, I couldn't hear it. It didn't matter. I was convinced that if I kept my head down, kept my mouth shut, stayed focused, stayed disciplined, made the sacrifices, and worked harder than anybody else, when the opportunity presented itself, I would be ready and strike hard.

I was not genetically gifted with astonishing talents. I don't come from a family of wealth. I make mistakes constantly. I lose focus. I procrastinate. I waste time. I feel pain. I experience fear. I bleed. I am not cut from a different cloth. I am not from another planet. I am a human, same as you, which means we have the ability to choose.

It doesn't matter what we do for a living, how much money we have in the bank, the size of our house, the disability we live with, who we care for, who cares for us, the car we drive, if we have a car at all, how popular we are, how much we can bench. *It. Does. Not. Matter.* We must simply decide. This is what I believe, this is who I am going to become, and I am willing to put it all on the line to achieve it.

Leave no chance to look back and wonder what if you had just pushed a little harder. Leave no chance for regret or to wonder what could have happened if you had done more with your life. Refuse average. Refuse mediocre. Refuse the status quo. Refuse to accept anything less than your very best. Right now, here and now, is where we make a stand. This is a choice we all have. Let's leave it all on the field.

Opportunities present themselves daily. We must see them and leverage them to propel our greatness, the greatness that exists within every single person on earth. It is sitting there right now, waiting to be released. A lion eager to hunt. Let it out. Enough is enough. Live life like you are the hero in your movie. You are the commander, and as your advisor, I recommend you proceed. Move.

Nick, Afghanistan, 2015

REVIEW — GENERAL TONY THOMAS

I FIRST MET NICK LAVERY in Wardak Province, Afghanistan in the fall of 2012. His team was operating in a remote area southwest of Kabul...at least 40km from any other coalition forces.

It was the occasion of his 2nd Purple Heart...he considered it a "minor wound." While presenting it to this giant of a man I made some joke about "let's make this the last Purple Heart you get." Of course, I could not know that the next time I'd see him he'd be literally fighting for his life in the ICU at Bagram AFB.

There are a lot of words that might describe Nick Lavery. While he is the epitome of a "Warrior" and the embodiment of human resilience, I think the word "indomitable" most aptly describes this extraordinary human being and his drive to overcome all obstacles.

"Objective Secure" is Nick's inspired study and description of what it takes to tackle life's challenges for all "warriors" not just those who are part of the military profession.

"Each of us struggles every day to define and defend our sense of purpose and integrity, to justify our existence on the planet and to understand, if only within our own hearts, who we are and what we believe in. We are all warriors." —*The Warrior Ethos* by Steven Pressfield

General Raymond "Tony" Thomas (Retired)
June 2, 2021

ACKNOWLEDGMENTS

I WOULD NOT BE HERE TODAY if not for the strength, sacrifice, and support of so many. Here are some, but certainly not all:

My parents, Michael and Terri—You brought me into this world. You stuck by me through countless mistakes. Thank you for believing in me.

My sister, Catherine—You were my first friend. Watching you grow into the person you are today has been one of life's greatest gifts. You're amazing and are among those I respect the most.

The Dustoff crew, Shank FST, and BAF staff—You saved my life. I will spend a lifetime trying to repay my debt to your service.

Doc JC Dallyrand and the Walter Reed staff—You kept me alive. Your existence proves angels do exist.

My strength coaches, Lance, Jason, Ray, and Jon—You are elite. Your value to our community cannot be measured.

My physical therapists, Kelly, Tara, and Teddy—You kept me in the game. Your ability to lovingly inflict pain is as impressive as it is sinister.

My fitness consigliere, Paul—You built the fitness foundation I stand on today. Your expertise is second to none. It is a privilege to call you a mentor and friend.

My SOCP teammates, Josh, Trey, and Jeff—You gave me purpose. Your tenacity on the mats pale in comparison to your character as men.

The 26 Vikings—You taught me the meaning of brotherhood. You gave me a second shot. Wherever, whenever, whatever for life. VoV.

The 35 Regulators—You are pirates. Among the best. Working for you is an honor.

LTG Beaudette and USASOC CAG—You were the icing on this cake. Thank you for your support and contribution.

GEN Thomas—You were there. You presented me all three of my purple hearts. And you have been a friend ever since.

The Horsemen of Precision Components, Eric, TJ, and Ray—You have the vision, heart, and skill necessary for greatness. We are just getting started. Lima Fox Golf.

Toni, Dom, and Vin—My heart. My soul. My why. I love you.

Made in USA - Kendallville, IN
34538_9780578352015
06.13.2023 1358